APR '98

Ready to Learn

How Schools Can Help Kids

Be Health

HEL
Reprint
Series

The HEL Reprint Series, begun in 1993, publishes books on topics of current concern to K-12 educators. The books' contents are drawn from articles that originally appeared in *The Harvard Education Letter,* a bimonthly publication of the Harvard Graduate School of Education that summarizes and interprets new research and innovative practice in K-12 education for practitioners.

Ready to Learn

How Schools Can Help Kids Be Healthier And Safer

Edited by
Edward Miller

THE HARVARD EDUCATION LETTER

HEL Reprint Series No. 2

Copyright © 1995 by President and Fellows of Harvard College.

Library of Congress Catalog Card Number 94-077728
ISBN 1-883433-01-0

The Harvard Education Letter
Gutman Library Suite 349
6 Appian Way
Cambridge, MA 02138

Cover design and typesetting: Sheila Walsh

Contents

Preface

Many people believe that public education has become a wasteful monopoly burdened by excessive bureaucracy, low standards, and cynical teachers. To many caring and intelligent citizens, the current system has become the problem, not the solution, and they yearn for the good old days when public education really worked.

Education *is* in serious trouble, but not because the public schools have fallen apart. Rather, schools are operating in a radically new environment, facing the triple burden of changed expectations, increasingly underprepared and troubled students, and new pressure to solve broad social problems.

Today, schools are being asked, appropriately, to prepare students to attain much higher levels of academic achievement. But at the same time, a larger proportion of children are coming to school without the essential prerequisites for success. If schools seemed better in the good old days, it is because many children were simply not being served by them. In 1950, less than 60 percent of children graduated from high school. Our high schools seemed better because they taught a select population—mainly white, motivated, and orderly youngsters with supportive parents.

Today's schools serve a growing number of children who are seriously at risk of educational failure because of poverty, poor health, inadequate nutrition, physical or sexual abuse, harassment, violence in their homes and neighborhoods, drug and alcohol abuse, and the depression and despair that so often overwhelm students who have suffered from trauma and neglect. How can children learn when they are hungry, hung over, or heartsick?

This collection of articles from the *Harvard Education Letter* on how we can promote students' physical and emotional health is intended to be a practical guide for educators and parents who are faced with these daunting problems. School administrators and teachers at all levels will find these essays both enlightening and empowering.

At the same time, we all need to think in broader terms about how children become educated, because schools by themselves cannot create an environment in which all children learn and thrive. We must enlist families, communities, businesses, churches, and other agencies to complement the educational mission of schools. If we expect universal achievement, of course we must concentrate on what goes on in the classroom. But we must also recognize that children learn outside school, and we must acknowledge that schools need partners in helping youngsters face today's challenges.

Jerome T. Murphy, *Dean*
Harvard University
Graduate School of Education

Introduction:
Not Ready to Learn

Edward Miller

The first of the six National Education Goals of 1990 stated that "by the year 2000, all children will start school ready to learn." Though it is unclear, in 1995, whether the United States has really made any progress toward this goal, the fact that policymakers are even talking about it may at least have served to promote an important truth: what happens to children in their lives outside of school and in their relationships with other people has a profound effect on their ability to benefit from education—on their readiness to learn.

The idea that students need to "start school ready to learn" applies to every youngster, every morning—not just to kindergartners on the first day of school. This notion may have seemed novel to politicians and the public in 1990, but it was no news to teachers, who must deal every day in their classrooms with the effects of a society that is often toxic to children.

The essays collected in this volume, all originally published in the *Harvard Education Letter* and updated for this edition, together lay out a disturbing picture of the risks to health and safety young people face today. Some are the direct result of poverty, in which one of every five American children now lives. Poverty can breed despair, domestic violence, poor nutrition, substance abuse, and reckless behavior.

But these issues of health and safety affect young people in all communities, and in middle-class and wealthy families as well as poor ones. Millions of children growing up without the support of secure, healthy relationships with adults are simultaneously bombarded by images of anger, aggression, mayhem, and murder, not only in the news but also in the movies, television shows, computer games, cartoons, and "action" figures promoted specifically for their entertainment. Educators trying to counter the effects of these influences in school-based conflict resolution programs often feel that their efforts are overwhelmed by the force of this commercial onslaught. Research confirms that such prevention programs, by themselves, are unlikely to change the behavior of young people raised in a culture so saturated with guns and images of violence.

Popular culture can be hazardous to children's well-being in other ways as well. Nutritionists struggle to promote healthful eating habits against the seductive and ubiquitous presence (even in many school lunchrooms) of fatty, salty, and sugary snacks and junk foods. Meanwhile, record numbers of children are overweight, 40 percent of five- to eight-year-olds exhibit at least one major risk factor for heart disease, and nearly half of all middle-school students are below minimum standards of physical fitness. At this critical point of early adolescence, many youngsters drop out of school and community sports activities, partly because of an overemphasis on competition. Again, a culture that defines success in sports as winning is part of the problem. At the same time, popular images of grotesquely thin fashion models and movie stars contribute to an epidemic of eating disorders among young women.

We're no better when it comes to sex. Young Americans receive ludicrously contradictory messages about sexuality: advertising and popular culture glamorize and exploit it; schools pretend it doesn't exist, or else treat it as a disease to be feared and avoided. Meanwhile, 78 percent of high school students are sexually active; 20 percent have had four or more partners. Almost every state now requires some kind of AIDS education in school, but knowledge is not translating into action. Kids may score high on tests about AIDS facts, but studies show that they are still unlikely to use condoms or to restrict their sexual activity to one partner known not to be HIV-infected.

Other research tells us that at least 20 percent of American females and between 5 percent and 10 percent of males are sexually abused in childhood by adults. Peer sexual harassment is rampant: 85 percent of girls and 76 percent of boys report being harassed at school; three out of five students admit having sexually harassed other students. Such behavior is becoming more common in the elementary grades, where adults are often at a loss to deal with or even recognize it. Few young people feel able to talk openly to their teachers about these problems. Only 10 percent of child abuse and neglect reports originate in schools; only 7 percent of the victims of harassment say they have told a teacher about it.

A clear side effect of abuse and harassment is lowered academic achievement. Victims of sexual harassment, for example, commonly report feelings of not wanting to come to school and finding it hard to pay attention in class.

Gay and lesbian students are particularly vulnerable to harassment, and in many schools abusive language and anti-gay slurs are tolerated. Faced with humiliation and rejection at home, at church, and in school, many gay young people succumb to depression and self-hatred. The rate of suicide among 15- to 19-year-olds has nearly tripled since 1960, and one study reports that about one-third of all teen suicides are gay and lesbian youth. Twenty-eight percent of gay and lesbian teenagers eventually drop out of school.

Any one of these symptoms of social sickness would be cause for alarm; together, they constitute a pandemic of crisis proportions. Teachers and school administrators are all too aware of the results of this sickness. Children who are abused, harassed, depressed, frightened, or hungry, who are abusing drugs or alcohol, or simply feeling sick and uncared for are not ready to learn in school. New standards, new curricula, new technology, and new national education goals will not make any difference to these students until their basic needs to be safe and well are addressed.

The solutions to many of these problems are well within our reach. We have good evidence now from model programs for sex education, drug abuse prevention, nutrition and health education, violence prevention, and, perhaps most important, comprehensive school-based health centers. The crucial question is whether we as a society are ready to learn from this knowledge—and to act on it.

We know that 90 percent of parents want their children to receive sex education in school, and that the most effective programs start in the early grades; yet fewer than 10 percent of students have access to this kind of comprehensive program. We know that prevention programs work best for adolescents when they promote open communication, trust, and peer leadership, and when adults serve as guides rather than authoritarian rule-givers; yet many adults continue to believe that the best way to get teenagers to behave is to lay down the law: just say no to sex, say no to drugs, say no even to depression. We know that sexually active young people who have access to school-based health clinics are more likely to use contraceptives and less likely to become pregnant; yet fearful adults continue to argue that such clinics encourage sexual activity (though there is no evidence that they do), and fewer than one percent of students are served by them.

Finally, we know that these are problems of society, not just of children and schools, and that they will be solved only with the collaboration and involvement of families, communities, government, business leaders, and educators. Yet many parents and community leaders blame the schools for failing to solve problems the schools did not create, and many demoralized and exhausted educators retreat into a defensive "that's not my job" attitude.

The good news is that where educators have taken a broad view of their duties to promote students' health and well-being and have found supportive allies outside the schools, they have created successful, replicable programs that are helping to make schools safer and children better able to cope with a dangerous environment. Many of these programs are described in the following pages, with names, addresses, and telephone numbers in the "For Further Information" listings at the end of each essay. If knowledge is power, then the combined knowledge of the researchers and practitioners whose work is the heart of this book can become a powerful force for change in our schools.

Part I:
Giving Kids
A Healthy Start

Most Schools Do a Poor Job of Promoting Students' Health

Adria Steinberg

P arents and teachers worry about the adolescents in their charge, and it is not hard to find reasons for concern. From the "breakfast" of chips and soda that many consume on the way to school to their seeming inability to concentrate on anything, adolescents appear to be hell-bent on testing the limits of good health and good sense.

At the same time, it is tempting to dismiss these worries. In the conventional wisdom, adolescence is a chronic (and sometimes acute) condition that time will probably cure. As many adults tell themselves, "they'll grow out of it."

While somewhat comforting, this view obscures an important change in the health status of teenagers. For the first time in this century, American adolescents are less healthy, less well cared for, and less prepared for life than their parents were at the same age.

What Ails Kids

The major causes of ill health, injury, and death among adolescents are accidents, homicide, suicide, and substance abuse. Other threats to their long-term health include poor diet, reckless sexual activity, and lack of exercise. One key reason for the declining health of American teenagers is that the cures for such "ailments" lie not in scientific or technological advances, but rather in emotional, behavioral, and social change.

How can teens learn to make sensible decisions in the face of conflicting messages? How can they learn to communicate their feelings and control their impulses?

In the past, notes Beatrix Hamburg of the Carnegie Council on Adolescence, children had opportunities to observe and practice such skills in family, apprenticeship, and community settings. Today, school is one of the only social contexts in which young people can systematically work on these skills with the guidance and support of adults.

Unfortunately, in most schools, this is not what happens. "Health" is usually offered in tandem with a physical education requirement. The course is limited in hours and didactic in pedagogy. A school may also sponsor sessions on such topics as AIDS, pregnancy, and drug abuse—what some educators refer to as the "disease of the month" approach.

Such programs may give teenagers important information about the nature of certain disorders or health problems. But they are unlikely to affect their attitudes, behaviors, and—perhaps most important—their motivation to seek out health-promoting environments.

Liverworts or Puberty?

In the fragmented curriculum of most middle and high schools, students see little connection between their health classes and their real concerns about their own changing bodies, or, for that matter, between their health and biology classes. A group of scientists and educators at Stanford University have set out to make these connections more apparent.

They have developed a two-year interdisciplinary course, the Middle Grade Life Sciences Curriculum, which is now being piloted in California schools. Students begin by learning about puberty. As Craig Heller, a Stanford biologist working on the project, points out, this is a subject of considerably greater interest and importance to young people than "the life cycle of liverworts and mosses"—a more typical starting point for a life sciences curriculum.

Heller criticizes most science texts for the middle grades as "well-illustrated vocabulary lists" that have excised any of the interesting concepts found in high school texts. Unlike traditional texts that offer, at most, a page or two explaining the reproductive system, the Stanford curriculum describes all of the biological changes associated with puberty and includes graphic illustrations of these changes.

The materials also focus on how it feels to go through puberty and on the social implications of the physical and emotional changes.

For example, students learn that weight gain at puberty is normal and healthy and need not be the occasion for concern or dieting.

Later units deal with sexuality, the reproductive system, sexual behavior, and maintaining sexual health. Students also learn about the extent to which institutions like marriage and family are culture-bound. During the second year, the curriculum includes a review of critical health problems.

The goal, explains Heller, is to use science to give students a knowledge base relevant to difficult decisions they may face. Information about biology and health is integrated with training in the life skills that will make young people socially competent, and with interactive exercises designed to foster sound decisionmaking.

Life Skills Training

Although social development is on the agenda of most schools, the teaching of social skills is usually not explicit, especially beyond the primary grades. The first districts to adopt life skills training tended to focus either on young children, in the hopes of inoculating them against problems, or on older adolescents already engaged in problem behaviors.

Today researchers emphasize the importance of the upper elementary and middle school years. It is at this age that many youngsters begin to feel pressure to participate in problem behaviors. At the same time, prevention is possible because the prevalence of such behaviors is still low.

Although there is no blueprint for effective prevention, consensus is emerging as to how to help teenagers stay healthy. Experts agree, for example, that prevention programs for young adolescents work best when they combine a generic approach with training in specific skills.

In other words, young people learn some of the general skills involved in social competence, such as how to enter into social situations, communicate their feelings, reduce stress, and control anxiety. At the same time, focusing on specific health issues like smoking or early, unprotected sex, they acquire information, skills, and strategies that will help them to make decisions and act on them in complicated and possibly conflict-filled situations.

Evaluations point to the value of active learning and of giving students opportunities to practice and apply new skills. Thus, unlike the traditional didactic methods of health education, life skills training relies on such methods as small groups, peer teaching or coaching, role-playing, and cooperative learning.

Another result of evaluations has been to make programs longer and more comprehensive: some now extend over more than a single school year or include boosters or follow-up sessions. And some programs offer training to administrators, counselors, and parents, as well as teachers, to ensure that children get the same messages from all of these adults in their lives.

When Help Is Near

Perhaps the most direct way in which schools can contribute to students' health is through collaborating with medical providers to establish school-linked health centers. Simply by its presence in or adjacent to the school building, a health center creates access to care for many adolescents who would otherwise not obtain the services they need.

Many adolescents cannot afford medical care, are uncomfortable or dissatisfied with the treatment they get, and do not know how to find appropriate services. In one typical school-based health center, described by Fred Hechinger in his book *Fateful Choices*, 38 percent of the clients reported that they would not have gone elsewhere for care or treatment and one-fourth said their only previous source of medical care had been hospital emergency rooms.

One telling statistic is that while almost half of the adolescents who are treated in traditional medical settings miss their scheduled return appointments, only 5.6 percent of those using school-related centers are reported to do so. In fact, nearly 30 percent of those who visit school centers develop a pattern of regular use.

Medical experts and educators agree that school-linked clinics are a promising innovation—with a potential that goes beyond addressing unmet health needs. Although evaluation data are still scarce, preliminary studies in several sites correlate use of the centers with declines in student absence and in smoking and drug use.

Why then have so few school-based centers been established? At this point, only about 500 school-linked centers are in operation, serving not even one percent of children between the ages of 10 and 19.

One key reason for this is that centers have become the focal point of community debate about birth control. Critics charge that easy access to birth control counseling and devices will cause a rise in sexual activity. Research has come up with no evidence of such an effect; and in one set of studies in Baltimore, the pregnancy rate among center users declined, while that of a control group continued to rise.

Controversies over birth control are only the most public of the barriers to establishing more health centers in schools. In addition, advocates for such centers face difficulties forging collaboration between health care providers and schools, and even greater difficulties obtaining stable funding.

Survive and Thrive

In the absence of adequate prevention programs or health services, youngsters adopt a narrow vision of health: health is how you feel "when you're not sick." In a comprehensive report on the status of adolescent health, the U.S. Office of Technology Assessment calls for a broader definition, arguing that being healthy during adolescence should mean more than the absence of a specific illness or chronic condition.

The issue is how to help teenagers not only survive but thrive in an increasingly complicated world. Perhaps the first step is for teachers, parents, and students to stop viewing health as something students "take" and to start exploring a broader question: how can we create an environment that promotes the long-term health and well-being of all the young people in our communities?

For Further Information

J. G. Dryfoos. *Adolescents at Risk: Prevalence and Prevention.* New York: Oxford University Press, 1990.

B. A. Hamburg. *Life Skills Training: Preventive Interventions for Young Adolescents.* New York: Carnegie Council on Adolescent Development Working Paper, 1990.

F. M. Hechinger. *Fateful Choices: Healthy Youth for the 21st Century.* New York: Carnegie Council on Adolescent Development, 1992.

National Commission on the Role of the School and the Community in Improving Adolescent Health. *Code Blue: Uniting for Healthier Youth.* Alexandria, VA: National Association of State Boards of Education; Chicago: American Medical Association, 1990.

U.S. Congress, Office of Technology Assessment. *Adolescent Health, vol. 1: Summary and Policy Options.* Washington, DC: Government Printing Office, April 1991.

What's for Lunch? A Menu for Changing What Schools Teach Children About Food

Edward Miller

While school reformers argue about outcome-based education, site-based management, and performance-based assessment, few researchers are asking students what *they* think most needs fixing in their schools. When they do ask, the answer, as often as not, is "the cafeteria food."

Ironically, the kids—and not the policy experts—may be the ones who have their priorities straight. Ample evidence suggests that what children learn about food and nutrition, especially in the early years, may have as profound an effect on their lives as any structural school reform. For those living in poverty—20.4 percent of U.S. children, according to a new UNICEF report—the stakes are particularly high, as the cycle of poor nutrition, poor health, and school failure repeats itself.

Some schools, meanwhile, have been quietly making impressive changes in their food and nutrition practices. They have reduced the proportions of fat and empty calories in their meals; involved families, students, and community agencies in designing and implementing nutrition education efforts; and turned their cafeterias into places where both kids and adults feel good about the food they're serving and eating.

At the same time, the Clinton administration has called for an abrupt about-face in the federal government's policies on school meals. Secretary of Agriculture Mike Espy announced in 1993 that the Reagan-Bush era policy of cutting the school lunch program was over, and that his department would move to reduce fat and salt and increase the amounts of fruits and vegetables in children's diets. School officials can expect a new federal emphasis on providing healthful food and more effective nutrition education.

In Love with Fat

Research on school lunches and children's diets suggests that America's love affair with greasy fast food may send many kids to an early date with death. Studies by the U.S. Department of Health and Human Services (HHS) show that today's children eat too much saturated fat and are heavier than kids were a generation ago, and that one child in four has an elevated blood cholesterol level. All three factors are associated with heart disease, the leading cause of death in the United States. Low-income and minority populations suffer far higher mortality rates from heart disease than higher-income or white populations, according to a 1990 HHS report.

School lunches are a big part of the problem. The Bogalusa Heart Study, a 15-year longitudinal study of Louisiana children by researchers at Tulane University, found that 40 percent of the calories in the kids' school lunches came from fat, 17 percent from saturated fat. Other research has consistently revealed similar levels, well above the limits of 30 percent and 10 percent, respectively, recommended by the U.S. Department of Agriculture (USDA). The Bogalusa Study also found that, over time, between 60 percent and 80 percent of the children exceeded the recommended daily intake of fat, saturated fat, cholesterol, and sodium, and that children with high cholesterol levels are more likely than the general population to have high levels as adults.

Very few children, meanwhile, are getting even the minimum recommended amounts of fruits and vegetables, which are excellent sources of vitamins, fiber, and potassium, and are low in fat, calories, sodium, and cholesterol. The National Research Council reports that a diet rich in fruits and vegetables helps reduce the risk of cancer and heart disease. But according to surveys by the National Cancer Institute and the USDA, only one child in ten eats five servings per day of these foods, the minimum recommended in the USDA guidelines. More than half of the children studied ate less than one serving (three ounces) of fruit per day, and almost two-fifths ate less than one serving of vegetables (other than potatoes, which were generally fried). One-third of the lunches chosen by children in the National School Lunch Program include no fruit or vegetables at all.

School menus reveal a striking lack of variety in fruits and vegetables. Almost half of the elementary schools in a USDA study offered only one choice of fruit or no fruit at all. Only 6 percent of the lunches included deep-yellow or dark-green leafy vegetables, which are important sources of beta carotene. Moreover, much of the fruit and vegetables served in school meals—such as tasteless canned green beans—is thrown away because the kids won't eat it.

Secretary Espy promised to double the amount of fresh fruits and vegetables offered to schools in the government's surplus commodities program, and to test reduced-fat cheeses and turkey sausages. Ellen Haas, USDA Under Secretary of Food, Nutrition and Consumer Services, is likely to push these reforms as well as better nutrition education programs. "There is no longer any question that diet is related to chronic disease," she says. To critics who object that fresh produce is more trouble for school cafeterias to store, prepare, and serve, Haas responds: "You have to find cost-effective ways to do it instead of throwing up your hands. It's not alien for kids to eat fruits and vegetables, but not when they've been cooked and recooked."

For many administrators, beset by the complex challenges of their jobs, school food is the last thing on their minds. Indeed, a growing number of districts are turning over their food service operations to private contractors. In other schools, where competition with local fast-food restaurants has cut into lunch revenues, financial pressure has led food service directors to change menus for the worse, nutritionally, and to offer students the same burgers, deep-fried chicken nuggets, corn dogs, chips, French fries, and soft drinks they might otherwise be buying down the street. Some schools even serve a commercial-brand "breakfast pizza" topped with sausage and gravy; almost 50 percent of the calories in this item come from fat.

Tastes Can Change

The experiences of other school systems, however, provide convincing evidence that kids will happily choose fresh fruits and vegetables, salads, whole-grain bread, and lower-fat meals if they're attractive, tasty, and well-prepared. Oklahoma City runs an aggressive nutrition education program in its 62 elementary schools. "We've been promoting fruits and vegetables," says Nutrition Education Coordinator Jean Carroll. "The kids love raw broccoli, cauliflower, and carrots with low-fat French dip. We've even started serving raw cabbage wedges with dip, and the kids are eating them."

Oklahoma City schools also now serve only whole wheat bread. "We started by making each sandwich with one slice of white and one of whole wheat, to get the kids used to it," Carroll says. "Now they don't even notice."

Many nutrition educators note that eating habits are formed early in life, and that elementary school programs are therefore critically important. An innovative program in the Chandler, Arizona, public schools suggests that a well-conceived classroom nutrition curriculum, coordinated with lower-fat menus in the cafeteria, will lead children to choose a healthier diet. The curriculum, "Heart-Healthy Lessons for Children," introduces students to the structure and function of the heart and to the risk factors—cholesterol and fat, sodium, smoking, and lack of exercise—that they can control themselves.

The Chandler program was tested in three of the district's twelve primary schools. Along with the lessons, the children got to taste-test new lower-fat items that school dietitians were developing for the lunch menu. "We tested a modified tuna salad recipe made with yogurt instead of pure mayonnaise," says Food Service Director Cathy McAlister, "and in the three schools where we were doing the program between 88 and 93 percent of the kids chose the tuna over the other lunch option—a peanut butter sandwich. In all nine of the other schools, the percentage who chose the tuna salad was much lower. So we knew the program was having an effect."

"Heart-Healthy Lessons for Children" was so well received in the Chandler public schools that it was published by the Arizona Heart Institute, which helped fund the original program. A revised 1994 edition of the curriculum is now available from the Institute.

Health Partners

Other school districts have formed partnerships with local health agencies to promote better nutrition for students. In Tennessee, the Memphis City Schools contracted with Methodist Hospital and the Shelby County Health Department to conduct health screenings in schools with the highest percentages of needy children. When tests indicate that a child has elevated blood pressure or cholesterol, according to Nutrition Services Director Shirley Watkins, "we send a letter home to the parents, telling them what the tests revealed and making suggestions for improving their diet."

Watkins has also made gradual changes in the school lunch menus: "We don't use butter, we serve skim chocolate milk, and we don't buy white bread anymore. We also changed the specifications for canned fruit to reduce the sugar." While some food service directors report that students have resisted the introduction of low-fat turkey franks, Watkins says she had no problems: "We substituted the turkey frank and I just didn't even mention it to anyone. Nobody noticed the difference."

Monitoring of the students' cholesterol shows that the Memphis program is having an effect. Tests revealed decreases in cholesterol in 20 percent of the children after six months.

A few innovative educators are using food service reform not only for health reasons but also to increase parent and community involvement. When Frank Mickens became principal of the huge Boys and Girls High School in the Bedford-Stuyvesant section of Brooklyn, New York, he made improving the lunchroom a top priority. He turned the cafeteria into a showplace, complete with well-stocked salad bars and a deli bar where students can make their own sandwiches with a wide variety of breads.

"We use food to bring the community into the school," Mickens says. "We have special breakfasts and dinners for the student of the month and to honor the kids' achievements, and we invite the parents and families. We often get a thousand people here for an honor-roll breakfast."

When he first came to the school, Mickens says, "lunchtime was when many kids would cut and get into trouble. Not anymore. Now they're so busy eating that we don't have problems in the lunchroom. If your cafeteria is good it affects other things. Food is significant in the totality of the school day."

For many students, what they eat in school may be the only or the best meal they get all day. "I know the kids," Mickens says. "I know which ones aren't getting enough to eat at home. I see to it that if they need to take a second or third sandwich, they get it."

In other schools, efforts to improve food and nutrition have been sparked by parents and students. Fran Schiffler, a parent in Springdale, Arkansas, got school officials to invite trainers from the American Cancer Society to show cafeteria staff ways to cook lower-fat meals. She organized the local PTA to staff a cafeteria taste-testing table where students could try new foods, and to purchase nutrition education materials for teachers and cooks.

Ed Benson, a parent activist in Miami, Florida, pushed his local school to offer whole-wheat hamburger buns and oat-bran waffles, and to replace ground beef with ground turkey. The experiment was so popular it spread to other schools in the Miami system.

The Guilford County Schools in North Carolina serve a variety of fresh fruits, juices, raw vegetables, and salads every day, and have been cited as a model of improved food service by the USDA. "We started the program several years ago with a committee of twenty concerned parents," reports Jean Reece, director of child nutrition services. "Then we formed a nutrition advisory committee in each school. There are parents in every school who want to make a difference. They know what their kids need and want. Now the kids here say that their favorite thing about school is lunch."

Food and Culture

Learning about good food is, for some kids, an entrée to a whole new world. Richard Schachter, a guidance counselor at Thomas C. Giordano Middle School in the Bronx, New York, runs an after-school cooking program for kids with poor attendance records. "We take advantage of the many cultures here—Italian, African American, Cambodian, West Indian—to explore an international menu," he says. "I take an item like rice, or dumplings, and we prepare it in different ways to see how it is a common element of many cuisines."

Schachter's class recently toured the kitchen at Le Cirque, one of the most elegant restaurants in Manhattan, at the invitation of its owner, Sirio Maccioni. "I wrote to him asking if we could come," Schachter says, "and he said yes. Part of the purpose of the visit was to let the kids see how professional chefs work—the pride and care they bring to it, how it makes them feel about themselves and about the clients they serve, how they approach cooking as an art, not just a job. The people in the kitchen were great to the kids. It was very special for them."

Schachter and other food-conscious educators share a common philosophy: if you care about your students, you have to pay attention to their diet and eating habits. His course is about more than just cooking: "Our mission is not just to make good food but to have a good experience together," Schachter explains. "We talk about the importance of sitting down together and sharing a meal after we cook. We set the table with real china, and we treat the meal as a celebration. Many kids today don't get to experience that aspect of eating together at home. I believe it's very important."

For Further Information

M. Bellinger et al. *Making Room on the Tray: Fruits and Vegetables in the National School Lunch Program.* 1993. Public Voice for Food and Health Policy, 1001 Connecticut Ave., NW, Washington, DC 20036; 202-659-6950.

Dietary Guidelines for Americans. Washington, DC: U.S. Dept. of Agriculture and Dept. of Health and Human Services, 1990.

R. Farris et al. "Nutrient Contribution of the School Lunch Program: Implications for Healthy People 2000." *Journal of School Health* 62, no. 5 (May 1992): 180-183.

Heart-Healthy Lessons for Children. Phoenix: Arizona Heart Institute; 800-345-4278. $25.

Nutrition Comes Alive: Food Service Worker Guide. Albany: New York State Education Dept., Bureau of School Food Management and Nutrition, 1989.

Organizing for Better School Food. 1991. Center for Science in the Public Interest, Children's Nutrition Project, 1875 Connecticut Ave., NW, Suite 300, Washington, DC 20009. $7.

Youth Sports: When Winning Is the Goal, Kids Are the Losers

Adria Steinberg

S tudies of the fitness of American youth tell a disturbing story. Many kids today are well on their way to becoming fully cooked couch potatoes, with all the attendant risks to their health.

For example, in a 1987 survey, 40 percent of the youngest age group (ages 5-8) evidenced at least one of the risk factors for heart disease: obesity, elevated blood pressure, or high cholesterol. In performance tests, one-third of the middle school boys and half the girls could not run a mile in ten minutes—a minimal acceptable level of fitness according to experts.

As many adults see it, television and Nintendo are the primary culprits. Some parents admit that their worries about the dangers of the streets or playgrounds make video addiction seem like the lesser evil. But physical education professionals do not accept the current levels of fitness as inevitable. They point to two places where kids could, but currently don't, develop the skills and habits for lifelong fitness—physical education classes in school and youth sports programs.

Washed Up at Ten

In almost all communities, physical education is a required part of the school program, at least through ninth grade. Budget cutbacks have meant larger classes, fewer hours, and itinerant teachers, but in most cases not the total elimination of gym classes.

In addition, many schools and communities offer organized, competitive sports programs for young people. In fact, despite the

concerns about fitness today, the trend in the 1980s was for enroll-
ment in sports programs to rise.

To some extent this statistical upswing may reflect the rising
number of young children (ages 5-7) and girls (particularly ages
8-10) who now participate. Nevertheless, these statistics indicate that
youngsters today, like those in previous generations, start out very
interested in sports.

But such participation peaks at around age 10 and then declines
throughout early adolescence. Why do so many kids drop out? In a
survey of 10,000 kids conducted by the Youth Sports Institute (YSI),
a state-funded research and training project housed at Michigan State
University, many explained their decision to quit with phrases like "I
wasn't having fun," "practices were boring," "no longer interested,"
or "took too much time."

The emphasis placed on competition, according to Vern Seefeldt
of YSI, is a key reason for this decline of interest and participation in
sports. In what Seefeldt terms the "elite model" of sports, success is
defined as winning.

This approach may foster a high level of skill development in a
few. But it does not help the majority of young people gain the
oft-cited benefits of participating in sports—such as learning movement skills that carry over to adulthood, gaining social skills, learning
the value of teamwork, and developing concepts of fair play.

Exercise More

Not surprisingly, early adolescence is also when many students
decide they don't enjoy gym. While they can't drop out of the class,
some begin to act out or engage in more subtle forms of resistance,
like forgetting to wear appropriate clothing or asking to visit the
nurse.

Although competition may not be as fierce in gym class as in
interscholastic sports, the elite model also affects the way such
classes are conducted. In the middle grades, much of the time is
devoted to learning the rules and moves of specific sports. In a typical
period, students may choose up or be assigned to a team and then
play a competitive team sport.

Many kids are "disenfranchised" by this system, according to
Charles Kuntzleman, the director of Fitness for Youth, a program
funded by Blue Cross and Blue Shield of Michigan in partnership
with the University of Michigan. Kids may decide they don't like

sports because they feel inadequate competing against more athletic classmates. And less adept players get few opportunities to improve their skills. In fact, in a typical 30-minute game a student may have only one or two chances to catch, kick, or throw the ball.

Perhaps the most serious problem with physical education programs that emphasize competitive sports is that no one gets much exercise. In an average gym class, Kuntzleman estimates, a student is actually in motion about 25 percent of the time. And only a few minutes of that motion are of sufficient intensity to develop healthy hearts and lungs.

More Balls, More Play

On the soccer field, 25 kids and 5 balls are in play. At one end of the field, a student has just scored a goal. She quickly retrieves the ball and brings it back to the center line for another try at dribbling and passing it down the field. There is no goalie and no score is kept.

This is the kind of soccer that Kuntzleman recommends to middle grade physical education teachers who attend Fitness for Youth workshops. Basketball can be similarly modified. With several balls in play, the tempo of the game increases and everyone gets plenty of exercise and numerous chances to practice the skills involved in handling the ball.

Some of the star athletes and their parents may not like it at first, Kuntzleman admits. But teachers who have been through his workshops have found that their own enthusiasm about this approach usually ends up carrying the day. Eventually, even the doubters see the advantages of getting to play more energetically and actively.

By modifying the games traditionally played at the middle school level, teachers can place the emphasis on physical fitness and motor skill development rather than on sports skills and winning. Fitness for Youth also provides teachers with aerobic workout routines targeted to grades 2, 5, and 7 and curriculum materials designed to raise the level of health awareness among children and their parents. More than 31 school districts in Michigan, representing 42,000 students, currently participate in the program.

Participating schools are encouraged to offer students—and their parents—a battery of fitness tests that will make it possible to chart their progress over a year. The battery includes biomedical tests for cholesterol, blood pressure, and body density, and performance tests, such as a mile run, curl-ups, and push-ups or pull-ups.

Coaches as Teachers

Interscholastic and community youth sports programs can also move away from the elite model, but only if more support and training are available to coaches. "There's a tendency for people to think that because they played the sport, they can coach it, but that's not so," cautions Seefeldt. "Our best estimate is that fewer than 10 percent of the youth coaches who need education are getting it."

YSI offers nine hours of training covering everything from how to organize good practice sessions to the complex motivational issues affecting a youngster's participation in a sport. A key target group for this training is the thousands of parents who become volunteer coaches each year because their children are on a team. The goals are to help them become more effective coaches and to reduce the high turnover rate.

Coaches, says a recent YSI report, need to be sensitive to psychological and emotional needs of youth, to be good communicators, and to understand the important developmental tasks of their young charges. It is striking that at a time when teachers are trying to become "more like coaches," fitness experts are calling for physical education teachers and coaches to view themselves more as educators.

For Further Information

Fitness for Youth. Charles Kuntzleman, Director, University of Michigan, CCRB, 401 Washtenaw, Ann Arbor, MI 48109.

C. Kuntzleman. "Is Your School in Shape?" *The Michigan Principal* 59, no. 2 (Spring 1988): 6-8.

D. Manuel. "Getting Kids in Shape." *Boston Globe* (December 1, 1991): 65-66.

V. Seefeldt, M. Ewing, and S. Walk. "An Overview of Youth Sports Programs in the United States." Washington, DC: Carnegie Council on Adolescent Development, 1991.

V. Seefeldt and P. Vogel. "What Can We Do About Physical Education?" *Principal* 70, no. 2 (1990): 12-16.

Youth Sports Institute. Vern Seefeldt, Director. 213 I. M. Sports Circle, Michigan State University, East Lansing, MI 48824.

Teaching Children About Sex

Adria Steinberg and Lisa Birk

Polls and surveys about sex education tell a consistent story: medical professionals, psychologists, teachers, parents, and students overwhelmingly believe that schools should be involved in teaching children about sex. Nine out of ten parents in national surveys want sexuality education in the schools, yet the current level of school involvement is minimal. Although 47 states either require or recommend sex education, "fewer than 10 percent of all children in America receive comprehensive sexuality education throughout their schooling," according to the Sex Information and Education Council of the U.S. (SIECUS).

The need for effective sex education is pressing. The percentage of all women age 15 to 19 who have had intercourse increased 23 percent between 1972 and 1990, and is now at its highest level in 20 years. Pregnancy rates are up. Young black women are especially likely to become pregnant early in life: 19 percent of 15- to 19-year-old African American women become pregnant, compared with 13 percent of Hispanics and 8 percent of non-Hispanic whites.

Income is perhaps the strongest predictor of pregnancy rates. The gap between first intercourse and first pregnancy among low-income teenagers is three years, compared with a gap of four-and-a-half years among higher-income adolescents. The good news is that sexually experienced adolescents are using contraceptives more. The Alan Guttmacher Institute found that two-thirds of teenagers use some form of contraception the first time they have sex. Overall, the pregnancy rate among sexually active teen women has declined. But because more young women are having intercourse, the number of pregnancies has continued to increase.

Americans are concerned about teenage sex: media campaigns target adolescent girls, and sometimes boys; feature articles profile high school moms; sex education classes exhort girls and boys to wait—or at least to use contraceptives. But "teen pregnancy" is not, strictly speaking, just about adolescent behavior. A California study found that men older than high school age accounted for 77 percent of all births among girls age 16 to 18, and for 51 percent of births among girls 15 or younger. *Vital Statistics of the United States* reports that 71 percent of all "teen" births involved an adult partner over age 20.

These new data on the likely age of the male partner in a "teen" birth may prompt a shift in thinking among educators. Underlying many sex education strategies is the presumption that pregnancy is the result of vulnerability to peer pressure, short-sighted thinking, lack of impulse control, and general rebelliousness. While those may be important contributing factors, the evidence suggests that teenagers who become pregnant are more likely to be victims of exploitative older males than simply "bad girls" who can't control themselves. It also suggests that the burden of "acting responsibly," so prominent in sex education curricula, should be shifted onto the shoulders of males more than females, where tradition and culture have historically placed it.

Whatever the content of sex education, many experts believe that decreasing unwanted pregnancies and the spread of HIV and other sexually transmitted diseases (STDs) requires a thorough, consistent, and repetitive approach. Educators advocate age-appropriate information for all students, beginning with kindergartners. Yet teaching about sex does not occur until seventh or eighth grade in many districts, and then only for a total of about eleven hours, as a small part of a year-long course—often health or biology.

What are the costs of waiting until middle school to introduce sex education? Does sex education change young people's behavior? How can schools best address the concerns of a small but vocal opposition? At a time of growing concern about AIDS and teenage pregnancy, such questions are emerging in more and more communities.

Start Early

The push for an earlier start in sex education is partly fueled by concern about sexual abuse and AIDS. Less dramatic, but perhaps more critical, is the decreasing age of sexual maturity. In the early 1900s, most girls began menstruating around age 14. Today, in industrialized countries, the average age is just over 12. Today's boys reach sexual maturity at 13. Because physical and emotional changes can begin two years earlier, many children have to deal with the onset of puberty before the age of 10.

According to Australian educators Ronald and Juliette Goldman, children as young as six are aware of and interested in sex differences, sexual relations, conception, and birth. But awareness does not always mean that children have accurate information. Interviewing children in five countries, the Goldmans found that most lacked—or were afraid to use—the basic vocabulary for discussing sex. For example, when they asked 9- to 11-year-olds to define *conception,* an English boy labeled it a "fluoride," an American girl said it meant "telling the future," and an Australian girl, "when you're knocked unconscious."

"How can you tell if a newly born baby is a boy or a girl?" asked the researchers. The children responded: "Because Mum dressed her in a dress. There's no other way to tell" (Australian girl, 7). "He [the doctor] looks through a magnifying glass into their eyes and he tells by the eyebrows" (American boy, 7).

"Do the bodies of boys and girls grow differently as they grow older?" was another question. A 5-year-old Australian boy answered, "Girls have hearts, boys haven't. Their hearts are in the stomach."

As the Goldmans point out, children avidly collect information. In the absence of facts, they will make up their own imaginative, often inaccurate theories. Adults may find these humorous, but many children hold on to these misconceptions and may suffer anxiety, embarrassment, or even lifelong consequences.

Older children may fill in their knowledge gaps with information from TV. According to one estimate, prime time shows depict 20,000 implied sex acts each year, often portraying affection and intimacy as synonymous with sexual intercourse. Commercials reinforce the message that happiness depends on looking, acting, and smelling sexy.

When asked how they learned about sex, many teenagers express anger. They are angry that parents and teachers are often either silent or authoritarian. As one young man told the *New York Times,* "They give us as examples the extremes of abstinence and promiscuity. But they don't tell us that there's something in between."

One consequence of adult silence is that children come to view sex as a furtive activity—and this may increase their vulnerability to sexual abuse. Over 80 percent of the 1,000 college students surveyed by the Goldmans recalled some kind of sexual experience with another person before the age of 12—usually in the form of childhood sex games, carefully hidden from adult view. Some children keep even bigger secrets. Experts agree that at least 20 percent of American women and between 5 percent and 10 percent of men were sexually abused in childhood by an adult (see "The Physically or Sexually Abused Child," page 91).

Even in schools where sex is discussed, there may be limitations on the conversation. The emphasis in many classrooms is on the biological and physiological aspects of sex. Curricular guidelines in some districts specifically restrict consideration of certain subjects (birth control, abortion, homosexuality), or instruct teachers to answer questions but not to open up controversial topics for discussion.

What is and is not said about sex in American schools is particularly detrimental to young women, according to Michelle Fine of the University of Pennsylvania. Analyzing public debates about sex education and school-based health clinics, as well as sex education curricula and classroom discussion, Fine describes what she calls "the missing discourse of desire." The underlying assumption is that the only choice females have to make is whether to say yes or no to the sexual demands of males.

Fine's own interviews and observations, however, reveal a much more complex picture. Girls are both excited and worried about actual or anticipated sexual relationships. In denying them opportunities to acknowledge and discuss their own desires, suggests Fine, schools may help to perpetuate their passivity and vulnerability to victimization. And this may lead to more, not less, teen pregnancy.

Sex "Just Happens"

Cross-national data collected by the Guttmacher Institute show that sexually active teens are much more likely to use contraception when they live in a society that accepts the reality of premarital sex and gives them the knowledge and equipment to experience it responsibly. Neither of these conditions is met in the United States. As a result, young people develop a simple and unfortunate line of reasoning: "It is wrong to have sex; therefore, I should not plan for it."

Even though American teens are comparable to European teens in their rate of sexual activity, the pregnancy rate among teenagers is five times higher in the United States than in other Western developed nations. Currently, 12 percent of all American women age 15 to 19 become pregnant each year. Unlike their European peers, American teens do not use birth control consistently. When asked to explain why, young people will say that they did not expect to have sex—that it "just happened."

Some American schools are responding to the challenge. Just a few years ago, most sex education programs began in ninth or tenth grade. Now many are starting earlier—though some critics say not early enough. And educators are trying different, more effective approaches, some wider in scope than others.

The latest curricula are based on the lessons learned over the past 20 years. In the mid-1970s, schools focused on decreasing the pregnancy rate by emphasizing the risks and consequences of sexual intercourse. Some students condemned the programs for being too "preachy." By the late 1970s, many schools de-emphasized risk and added "values clarification" and communication skills to the curriculum. Studies revealed that both approaches had limited impact. Both increased student knowledge, but, researchers discovered, knowledge is only weakly connected to behavior. According to Douglas Kirby, research director at Education Training Research (ETR) Associates in Santa Cruz, California, neither program "measurably reduced teenage pregnancy; at best, they may have slightly increased the use of birth control."

With the identification of the AIDS virus in 1985 and the failure of previous education efforts, a third type of curriculum appeared. These programs emphasized abstinence and often excluded discussion of contraception or "safer sex." Evaluations showed that students became less accepting of premarital sex in the short term. But according to Kirby, "evaluations indicate that the programs did not delay intercourse or reduce frequency of intercourse."

The "fourth generation" of sex education programs, as Kirby calls them, are a synthesis of the previous three, a combination of factual information and values support with decision-making and communication skills. The best of them are positively affecting teens' sexual choices. The Guttmacher Institute reports three measurable results: Some participants delay the initiation of sexual intercourse—in one study, for up to seven months. Participants are more likely—13 percent to 50 percent more in three evaluated programs—than those in control groups to use condoms and other contraceptives. Finally, higher proportions of participants than control-group members maintained monogamous relationships and fewer had high-risk partners after the intervention.

Successful interventions, claim the authors of the 1994 Guttmacher booklet *Sex and America's Teenagers,* share a number of characteristics: a narrow focus on reducing specific behaviors, a chance to practice new skills through role play and simulations, reinforcement of group norms about unprotected sex that are age- and experience-appropriate, and education about peer and social pressures.

Theory into Practice

The programs documented as most successful are based on two theories: social learning theory and social inoculation. Social learning theory posits that people learn by observing others' behavior and then practicing those skills. Many schools use modeling and role play to demonstrate and teach communication skills. Social inoculation resembles physiological inoculation: people can fight off peer pressure when they can identify the tactics. After brainstorming a list of common "lines," a class might strategize and then act out ways to avoid intercourse or unwelcome sexual advances.

One program with a narrow focus and a chance to practice new skills is Postponing Sexual Involvement (PSI), a curriculum adopted by California's Governor Wilson in 1991 to decrease teen pregnancy rates. With a slogan of "Education Now and Babies Later" (ENABL), PSI has targeted two groups: 12- to 14-year-olds and the community of adults. The curriculum teaches three assertiveness techniques for avoiding sexual contact: just say no without an excuse; reversing the pressure ("Sam, why do you keep trying to kiss me when you know I said no?"); and hanging up or leaving the room. The students are then given opportunities to practice the strategies over five hours of interactive instruction.

The ENABL campaign sees the news media as an essential component. It has produced public service announcements to educate and elicit support and involvement from the community. "ENABL is a campaign," says Judith Pratt, chief of health education in California.

"It's got balloons, shoelaces. It's got hype." And hype, she believes, is critical to the success of the program. "Change the individual and at the same time change the environment," says Pratt. "It works. The best example is the change in smoking behavior. You've got no-smoking ordinances, insurance incentives—you've got the cohesiveness of a single message. Now imagine a kid learning assertiveness techniques, and then going home to see a P.S.A. with the same message. I love it when I hear a kid use a line they heard on television."

Although the effects of the California curriculum are not yet known—the first independent evaluation should be available in 1995—critics have already weighed in. Some researchers believe that abstinence programs may not reduce the spread of STDs because they leave out important information on preventive measures and leave sexually active teenagers more at risk. Pratt responds that sexually active teens receive sexual health information in middle school biology classes. Furthermore, she argues, "ENABL is preventing STDs. Because if you're not having sex, you're not getting or spreading STDs."

Some students are critical, too. PSI reports in a 1994 survey that the majority of students liked the program, but 82 percent requested more information on the transmission and prevention of STDs and HIV.

Another skills-oriented program, called Enhancing Skills to Prevent Pregnancy, discusses an array of options from abstinence to safer sex. The curriculum, developed by ETR Associates, focuses on helping teenagers learn to make and communicate decisions about contraception. Students read vignettes and participate in role play about teenagers like themselves who are trying to decide "how far to go," and then find ways to communicate that decision clearly and politely. Homework also requires active learning: assignments include interviewing their parents (after predicting what they will say about abstinence and birth control), pricing contraceptives in a drug store, and visiting a clinic.

The program is based on a curriculum created in 1981 by Stephen Schinke and his colleagues. Students who participated in Schinke's classes had better problem-solving and communication skills, more knowledge of reproduction and birth control, more favorable attitudes toward contraception, and more diligent contraceptive practice than did a control group of students. Researchers were unable to determine, however, if the program had any effect on pregnancy, birth, STD, or HIV rates.

SIECUS promotes a more comprehensive approach with a few basic goals: sex education in all grades from kindergarten through high school; inclusion of all topics at the appropriate grade level; a balance of abstinence and safer sex messages for adolescents; and direct answers about sexual issues in adolescent programs. The emphasis is on preparing children of all ages for good personal relationships, characterized by a sense of responsibility and concern for others. Several U.S. communities use this approach, offering "family life education" programs in schools.

In Alexandria, Virginia, for example, when primary grade children first learn to "name and claim" their body parts, they also discuss the importance of respecting one another. The focus is on gender similarities as well as differences. As they move into the middle grades, children learn more about the reproductive system, and also explore such topics as sex roles in the family and the workplace, and how the media deal with sex. In ninth grade, all students take a full-year course that places sexuality in the context of human development. In the eleventh and twelfth grades, students take a two-day course in the transmission and prevention of STDs and HIV that includes a day of medical information and a discussion with a panel of HIV-positive men and women.

The Pregnancy-Poverty Equation

Joy Dryfoos, formerly of the Guttmacher Institute and now an independent researcher, believes that neither the skills-oriented nor the comprehensive approach goes far enough. It is not enough, she argues, for teenagers to have information and decision-making skills. They need a reason not to get pregnant, she says. They need opportunity. Education and jobs, Dryfoos believes, would give teens the incentive they need to use contraceptives more consistently or to defer sex until career goals are further along.

Most people, Dryfoos asserts, have the pregnancy-poverty equation backward. It's not that teen pregnancy causes poverty. "Most people who become teen mothers are poor before they become mothers," she says. "The prevention of pregnancy is related to the prevention of poverty."

Children of poor families are significantly more at risk for substance abuse, pregnancy, and delinquency. Dryfoos estimates that one in four children age 10 to 17 in the United States "does it all"—uses drugs, has early unprotected intercourse, and is truant. She advocates a whole-child, whole-family approach to alleviate the impact of poverty: centralizing social services in schools. Such "full-service schools" would provide high-quality education while social service agencies would offer a wide array of services from dental care and adult literacy programs to welfare payments and family planning and counseling.

Dryfoos acknowledges that most communities are a long way from providing full-service schools, but she cites two exemplary programs, one in New York and one in California, in her 1994 book, *Full Service Schools: A Revolution in Health and Social Services for Children, Youth, and Families.* While "neither [school] is fully realized yet," she writes, "both appear to be committed to bringing in whatever the students need to make it," including help with food, housing, job skills, and English as a second language. And, she points out, the average cost for full services is $500 to $1,000 per student per year, "bringing the total expenditure per child in disadvantaged, underfunded school districts closer to the amount spent in more privileged areas."

The number of school-based clinics is growing. Of the 82,000 public schools operating in 1991-1992, slightly more than 500 had school-based health centers, up from 327 in the previous year. There is wide support for them. A 1988 Harris poll found that 73 percent of Americans favor making birth control information and contraceptives available through such clinics.

Moreover, students use the clinics. One recent survey found that 18.5 percent of all eligible students visited the clinics for sexual health needs, 26 percent for preventive services, 20 percent for mental health services, and 31 percent for acute care. Nearly 40 percent of all clinic users were uninsured.

While critics argue that school-based clinics may encourage sexual activity, there is no evidence that they do. There is evidence, however, that students who use clinics are more likely than their peers to use contraceptives if they are sexually active, and less likely to become pregnant. Furthermore, an evaluation of a school-based education and health clinic program in Baltimore found that students postponed first intercourse by an average of seven months, compared with peers who were not exposed to the program. Another encouraging finding is that efforts to involve boys paid off. The highest rate of increase in the use of birth control was among junior high males.

But Do They Work?

Whether the experts endorse a more limited program or the full-service model, all acknowledge problems in assessing the effectiveness of any one approach. Few longitudinal studies measuring long-term impact exist. Many studies have been conducted without control groups. And a large majority of studies rely on self-reporting—a notoriously flawed method.

Some evaluations do use external data such as schoolwide or countywide birth rates and abortion rates to measure program efficacy. But, according to the Guttmacher Institute, "schoolwide rates have been shown to fluctuate widely from year to year, . . . and countywide rates may be based on a pool of adolescents that is much larger than the group of teenagers participating in the program, which would dilute the effect of a program operating only in one school."

The most reliable studies consistently conclude that the most effective programs combine sex education with interactive instruction, highlighting responsible behavior and decisionmaking skills.

At this point, too much of what is known about sex education is being ignored in the name of political expediency. Schools provide more programs than they used to, but still too little, too late. Districts offer sex education without providing enough funds for curriculum development or teacher training; they mandate AIDS education but forbid any mention of condoms; and they sponsor school-based clinics that cannot prescribe birth control.

Some communities have managed to move beyond such compromises and institute innovative, comprehensive programs. How have they done it? It is possible to pinpoint two key elements:

- *Teacher training.* In a recent national survey of teachers, the Guttmacher Institute found that teachers want to be well prepared before moving into the controversial terrain of sex education. "People are not necessarily comfortable talking about sex with children," notes Claire Scholz, the family life education coordinator in Irvington, New Jersey. In both the

Irvington program and the one in Alexandria, Virginia, teachers receive special preparation. By the time they teach their first lessons, they are not only secure in their factual knowledge but also have had chances to clarify their own values and to practice an open, accepting attitude.

- *Parent and community involvement.* Family life educators emphasize the importance of involving parents and other local citizens in every step of the process. Hearing from a range of people, those running the program can quickly address emerging concerns and foster community support.

Parents of middle school students, for example, may need assurances that their children will not have their privacy invaded, or that the curriculum will not assume that "everyone is doing it." Over time, trust increases, and even a parent who started out wanting to restrict conversation about particular topics (such as abortion) may realize that teachers can handle such discussions with sensitivity to the strong beliefs of different religious and cultural groups.

It is also important, says Jean Hunter, the former coordinator in Alexandria, for parents to know that they can keep a child out of the program if they wish. In fact, less than 5 percent of parents opt out in most places—an indication of just how widespread is the support for sex education.

For Further Information

Alexandria Public Schools Family Life Education Program. Cathy David, curricular/staff development specialist, 2000 North Beauregard St., Alexandria, VA 22311.

J. Dryfoos. *Full Service Schools: A Revolution in Health and Social Services for Children, Youth, and Families.* San Francisco: Jossey-Bass Publishers, 1994.

Enhancing Skills to Prevent Pregnancy. ETR Associates, P.O. Box 1830, Santa Cruz, CA 95061-1830.

M. Fine. "Sexuality, Schooling and Adolescent Females: The Missing Discourse of Desire." *Harvard Educational Review* 58, no. 1 (February 1988): 29-53.

A. Gambrell and D. Haffner. *Unfinished Business: A SIECUS Assessment of State Sexuality Education Programs.* SIECUS (130 W. 42nd St., Suite 2500, New York, NY 10036; 212-819-9770), 1993.

R. Goldman and J. Goldman. *Show Me Yours! Understanding Children's Sexuality.* New York: Penguin Books, 1988.

D. Kirby, R. Barth, N. Leland, and J. Fetro. "Reducing the Risk: Impact of a New Curriculum on Sexual Risk-Taking." *Family Planning Perspectives* 23, no. 6 (November/December 1991): 253-263.

M. Males. "Poverty, Rape, Adult/Teen Sex: Why 'Pregnancy Prevention' Programs Don't Work." *Phi Delta Kappan* 75, no. 5 (January 1994): 407-410.

Judith Pratt, Chief of Health Education, State of California, Department of Health Services, 714/744 P St., P.O. Box 942732, Sacramento, CA 94234-7320.

Sex and America's Teenagers. Alan Guttmacher Institute (120 Wall St., New York, NY 10005), 1994.

Part II:
Preventing
Risky Behavior

Beyond the Condom Wars: A Comprehensive Approach to AIDS Education

Susan Eaton

Earvin "Magic" Johnson's public statement that he had contracted HIV, the virus that causes AIDS, loosed a torrent of questions not only to hotlines but in classrooms as well. Many teachers, whether or not they were already teaching state-prescribed AIDS curricula, felt a new moral mandate to talk more explicitly about the disease and how to prevent it.

The media frenzy that followed Johnson's announcement has died down, but the crisis continues unabated. Adolescents continue to be at high risk of contracting HIV. The Washington-based Center for Population Options, a nonprofit research group, estimates that 78 percent of young people ages 15 to 19 are sexually active and that more than 20 percent of high school students have had four or more partners. Recent research indicates that adolescents are still unlikely to use condoms or to restrict their sexual activity to one partner who is known not to have HIV.

The evidence also suggests that HIV is spreading among teens. Of the 289,300 cases of full-blown AIDS reported to the Centers for Disease Control (CDC) as of March 1993, 1,167 involved people ages 13 to 19—an increase of 681 cases since March 1990.

More significantly, one-fifth of all AIDS victims are in their twenties, according to the CDC. Given the seven-to-ten-year incubation period for the disease, many of these patients must have been infected in their teens. The rate of infection is higher for African American and Latino teens than for other groups: blacks account for 37

percent of reported teenage AIDS cases, Latinos 19 percent. Runaways and homeless youth are also at high risk.

Risky Business

The question facing educators is no longer whether to teach
about HIV and AIDS, but how. While 48 states now require AIDS
education in school, studies suggest that knowledge is not translating into action. In other words, students may score high on tests
about how HIV is contracted, but they still are not using condoms or
abstaining from sexual intercourse in appreciable numbers. While
condom use has risen among teens since the 1970s, a 1989 survey
showed that nearly one-half of the teenage males had not used a
condom when they last had intercourse.

The prevalence of sexually transmitted diseases such as gonor-
rhea and herpes among teens also is proof that they are persisting in
risky behavior. The CDC estimates that one out of four teenagers will
contract a sexually transmitted disease before graduating from high
school. Studies show that adolescents feel invulnerable not just to
AIDS but to all types of danger and therefore may be less likely to take
precautions against the disease.

These troubling facts have led a growing number of educators
and public health officials to talk more openly about condom use or
safe "sexual alternatives" that stop short of intercourse or oral sex.
Joycelyn Elders, former surgeon general, is an outspoken advocate
of providing condoms to students, and public schools in New York
City, Baltimore, Houston, Chicago, Portland, Oregon, and a growing
number of other districts are doing just that.

"If you look at it from a public health perspective and put aside
the political ramifications," says Devon Davidson, director of the
AIDS education project for the National Coalition of Advocates for
Students, "it's hard to come down on any other side than making
condoms easily available. We're talking about saving kids' lives."

How to Teach About AIDS

Though there is no conclusive evidence about what kind of
teaching is most likely to get young people to change their sexual
behavior, sex education experts, psychologists, and health professionals propose the following guidelines:

Personalize the information. For AIDS education to be effective it
has to do more than simply teach biological facts. Good programs

acknowledge the social and psychological barriers to prevention in a teenager's world. Educators must recognize not only that students may be pressured into sex by peers but also that openly admitting to sexual activity can be humiliating for some young people.

Classroom role-playing that creates realistic scenes of teenage life can be especially useful. For example, students might act out a scene in which a boy enters a drug store to buy condoms for the first time. Another skit might involve a girl who chooses to end a relationship in which her partner refuses to use a condom or have an HIV test. Role-plays like these, according to University of Western Ontario psychologist William A. Fisher, provide students with "scripts" they can use in their own social settings.

Another teaching technique encourages adolescents to make decisions about hypothetical sex-related situations and then makes them "live with" those decisions later on. In one such classroom game, a young man who decides to have casual sex in the first round of the game may have a child to care for by the sixth round, limiting his options about college or travel. This, Fisher explains, helps young people see how spur-of-the-moment decisions can affect the future.

Promote healthy attitudes toward sexuality. Effective AIDS education encourages students to think of their sexuality in a healthy, guilt-free way. Explicit talk about arousal, desire, and sexual activities that don't transmit HIV—such as genital touching—is essential. Abstinence, the best way to avoid HIV infection, should be part of the curriculum, but simply advocating abstinence is not enough. The discussion should be free of moralistic overtones that imply that it is always wrong to have sex.

Educators who choose to stress abstinence are well advised to start AIDS education in the early grades. Encouraging students to delay sex is effective only if the discussion takes place before they are sexually active—in elementary school, or middle school at the latest.

Debra Haffner, executive director of the Sex Information and Education Council of the U.S., a nonprofit research and advocacy group, recommends that discussion of abstinence focus on helping teens learn the negotiating and decisionmaking skills that will give them strength to say no. Just telling adolescents to say no to sex doesn't work. Some health educators promote what is called the ABC's of AIDS education: Abstinence, Be monogamous, and Condoms.

AIDS education is probably most effective when offered as part of a comprehensive, open discussion about sexuality. Cross-national data collected by the Alan Guttmacher Institute show that sexually active teens are more likely to use contraception when they live in a society that accepts the fact of premarital sex (see "Teaching Children About Sex," p. 21).

Involve the community. Education about HIV and AIDS should not be limited to the classroom. The most effective programs appear to be those whose messages are reinforced by local clergy, community and business leaders, hospitals, youth agencies, and news media. Many educators recommend that all facets of a community help plan and implement an HIV-prevention strategy aimed at adolescents. Though explicit talk about AIDS prevention, sexuality, and condoms usually inspires controversy and vocal opposition, many districts have successfully implemented programs by involving the community and educating parents before and during the effort.

HIV at School

More and more school officials across the country are dealing with the medical, legal, and ethical issues raised by the presence of an HIV-infected student or staff member. Although numerous studies have now clearly proved that the AIDS virus cannot be transmitted by casual, everyday contact, many adults and children still react with worry and fear to the news that someone at school has HIV. People with HIV or AIDS have in many cases been unnecessarily barred from classrooms and workplaces—a reaction that is both a violation of their legal rights and, often, a public relations nightmare for the school and community.

School administrators and health officials need to be prepared for such situations, which are sure to occur with increasing frequency in the coming years. Promoting the humane and ethical treatment of people with HIV goes hand in hand with effective AIDS education in the classroom.

The National Association of State Boards of Education publishes a guide to developing policies for students and staff members who are HIV-infected. It contains essential information and advice about the difficult responsibilities administrators face—including evaluating the medical condition of infected persons to determine the proper classroom or job placement, deciding who in the school community needs to know a person is infected, dealing with the fear of HIV infection through biting (the risk is virtually nonexistent), deciding whether to require an HIV test if they suspect that a student or staff member is infected (in a word, no), and managing a crisis brought on by an alarmed group of parents.

Students Take a Stand

The threat of AIDS has inspired many students to pressure school boards and even state legislatures to enact policies to protect them. Formal education, many teens say, is not enough.

At Brookline High School in Massachusetts, student government leaders worked for a year on a campaign to allow condoms to be distributed at their school. The school board turned down the request, but formed a task force to study the issue. After a year of research and difficult negotiations, the board went along with the task force's recommendations to make condoms available and to train fifteen teachers and health personnel to counsel students when they get condoms for the first time.

There are no studies that prove that giving students condoms in school either reduces unsafe sexual behavior or increases overall sexual activity, as critics fear. But many health professionals and educators believe that even the chance that it will help prevent the spread of HIV is worth the public controversy such proposals provoke.

In Connecticut, students from Stamford High School led a successful statewide lobbying effort to make HIV testing available to minors. The campaign, which led to repeal of a rule that required parental permission, was born out of the increased awareness about the disease after Magic Johnson announced that he had tested HIV-positive. The effort was widely supported by teachers, administrators, and health professionals across the state.

Teenagers as a group are more easily influenced by peers than by adults. Thus sex education programs may be most effective if the students themselves help develop the curriculum, give presentations, or create lesson plans. The Center for Population Options, in a review of the research on the effectiveness of sex education, suggests that "when many student leaders openly and consistently express norms against risk-taking behavior, schoolwide norms may, in fact, change."

For Further Information

Centers for Disease Control. *Guidelines for Effective School Health Education to Prevent the Spread of AIDS.* Atlanta: U.S. Department of Health and Human Services, 1988.

J. Collins and P. Britton. *Training Educators in HIV Prevention: An Inservice Manual.* Santa Cruz, CA: ETR Associates, 1991. Sample agendas for one- and two-day seminars for training teachers to educate children about AIDS. 800-321-4407.

National AIDS Information Clearinghouse. P.O. Box 6003, Rockville, MD 20850. 800-458-5231. Materials available in English and Spanish.

National Association of State Boards of Education. *Someone at School Has AIDS.* Alexandria, VA, 1989. 703-684-4000.

M. Quackenbush and S. Villarreal. *Does AIDS Hurt? Educating Young Children about AIDS.* Santa Cruz, CA: ETR Associates, 1992. 800-321-4407.

Reducing the Risk: A School Leader's Guide to AIDS Education. National School Boards Association, 1680 Duke St., Alexandria, VA 22314; 703-836-6722. $7.25.

Steps to Help Your School Set Up an AIDS Education Program. National Coalition of Advocates for Students, 100 Boylston St., Suite 737, Boston, MA 02116; 617-357-8507. $3.

Drug and Alcohol Education: What Works

Adria Steinberg and Lisa Birk

Illicit drug use among adolescents is on the decline. In 1983, 62.9 percent of twelfth graders reported that they had experimented with drugs at least once. A decade later, according to the National Clearinghouse for Substance Abuse Prevention, the number of high school seniors who had tried illegal drugs had dropped by 20 percent, down to 42.9 percent. Substance abuse is still a significant problem, but the downward trend has some experts excited.

Nancy Tobler of the State University of New York believes that a variety of factors are helping today's youths avoid drugs. She examined 91 treatment programs and discovered that successful ones matched the method of instruction to the developmental needs of the age group. Tobler asserts that we now know what works for most teens. (Her report did not focus on the needs of "abusive or compulsive adolescent drug users," an estimated 10 percent of the teenage population.)

Middle-grades students, according to Tobler, were best served by a highly structured, skill-focused curriculum. The shorter programs taught students how to deal effectively with peer pressure using peer modeling, role play, and videotapes. The longer programs, usually about 20 hours, addressed interpersonal skills and issues of self-confidence. Students practiced communication skills, assertiveness techniques, solving problems, and setting goals. The longer programs were effective in reducing tobacco, alcohol, and marijuana use; the shorter curricula inhibited tobacco smoking only.

High school students were better served by 10-to-12-session programs that used small groups to share ideas, feelings, and experiences. The most successful leaders, often mental health professionals, established trust and facilitated communication by taking a nonauthoritarian stance.

All adolescents benefitted from peer leadership, interactive learning, and programs that concentrated on just one illegal substance. Preventing alcohol abuse continues to be the most difficult challenge, Tobler's research showed.

No Consensus

Many experts believe that adult attitudes and behavior influence young people's choices. Since alcohol is the most widely used and most acceptable dangerous drug, teenagers are more likely to drink excessively than to smoke or use other illegal drugs. Even the most successful programs have little impact on the teen drinking problem.

Although the 10 percent of teens who are serious substance abusers were not the focus of her study, Tobler believes that at-risk populations profited most from alternative programs "designed to produce personal competence and give an individual a sense of control over his environment." Such programs often use individualized activities like physical adventure and career planning and preparation.

Other researchers are less sanguine. Wayne Harding, director of operations at Social Science Research and Evaluation (SSRE) in Burlington, Massachusetts, thinks Tobler's conclusions are wrong. "She primarily focuses on changes in knowledge and attitude, not on behavior," he says. "We do not have a list of the five best ways to prevent substance abuse. This isn't like heart disease, where you can say, 'If you cut down on cholesterol, you're statistically better off.' "

Harding believes there are two barriers to finding definitive answers to the question, "What works?": defining the problem, and assessing the solutions. Substance abuse, he asserts, varies with population and region: "It looks different in Framingham, Massachusetts, than it does on an Indian reservation, so solutions may look different from community to community." And before a community can tackle the problem of illegal drug use, it must agree on the definition of the problem. "What are you trying to prevent?" Harding asks. "*All* drug use? Abuse only? Break-ins? Casualties?" Different definitions, he says, require different solutions.

After identifying the problem and devising a strategy, the only way a community can figure out if it is working is through careful evaluation of the results. But evaluating drug abuse prevention programs in a valid, scientific way is notoriously difficult. "Control groups are expensive," Harding notes. "And no community wants a control group because then those people aren't getting any help. It's also very expensive to do long-term follow-up studies. How long do you follow them?"

Another problem is that meaningful tests of a program's effects are difficult to design and execute. How do you reliably measure what a particular student will do when offered crack at a party? Follow him around everywhere he goes?

In the few cases where long-term controlled studies have been conducted, the results are hardly promising. An analysis of eight evaluation studies of Project DARE (Drug Abuse Resistance Education), which is by far the most popular and widespread school-based drug education program in the United States, found that it has only a very small, short-term effect on students' drug use.

Learning from Our Failures

Still, many experts agree that we learned from our failures in the 1970s and 1980s, and kids today are better off. Fifteen years ago most programs either delivered information about drugs and alcohol or painted a dire picture of the consequences of substance abuse. Neither approach was effective in altering students' behavior or intentions to use drugs in the future, according to a review of 127 such programs offered by schools between 1968 and 1977.

The next round of programs, with a more general focus on strengthening students' senses of responsibility and self-esteem, also were not effective. For example, a five-year study of elementary and junior high schools in Napa, California, found strategies such as cross-age tutoring and operating a school store to be no more effective than the conventional drug education course in changing drug-related attitudes, intentions, or behavior.

As with sex education (see page 21), substance abuse education falls into three general categories: narrow, short-term programs that teach refusal skills; slightly longer-range programs that teach refusal skills and increase assertiveness; and programs that combine all of the above with community involvement. A fourth and relatively rare approach is embodied in Joy Dryfoos's concept of the "full-service school" (see page 29). Because children living in poverty are significantly more at risk, not just of substance abuse but also pregnancy, suicide, and delinquency, Dryfoos believes we need to treat all the problems under one roof: the school's. The full-service school, she argues, would decrease the number of dropouts and ultimately increase the number of healthy, self-sustaining adults.

Over the last decade, several programs have achieved some promising results, particularly in deterring smoking. Tobler found that tobacco programs were "extremely successful" regardless of the strategy employed. But the most effective ones concentrated on tobacco, rather than endorsing a wider anti-drug message.

It may be very important to start anti-smoking programs early. The U.S. Department of Health and Human Services (HHS) reports that the "initiation of daily smoking most often occurs in grades six through nine." And several other reports, including one by Dryfoos in 1990, demonstrate that cigarettes and alcohol serve as "gateway" drugs—that is, most adolescents who go on to use illegal drugs begin with legal substances.

Whatever the approach, taking adolescent psychology into account is critically important. Focusing on the immediate negative consequences of smoking—smelly breath and clothes, the possibility of peer disapproval—is more effective than talking about the threat of lung cancer in some nebulous future.

Most adolescents experiment with alcohol. According to a 1992 HHS study, 69 percent of eighth-graders, 82 percent of tenth-graders, and 88 percent of twelfth graders have tried alcohol. Heavy drinking, however, has been on the decline—though it is still widespread. The monthly prevalence of drinking among high school seniors decreased from 72 percent in 1980 to 51 percent in 1992, and the reported rate of drinking five or more drinks in a row during the previous two weeks dropped from 41 percent in 1983 to 28 percent in 1992.

Overall, illegal drug use among adolescents is also down. HHS found that 27 percent of high school seniors admitted using illegal drugs in 1992, half the peak level of 54 percent in 1979. Eighth-graders, however, showed a "significant increase" in the use of marijuana, cocaine, LSD, and hallucinogens other than LSD. Researchers theorize that, as the drug epidemic subsides and there are fewer opportunities to learn of the hazards of drugs from friends, there is a danger of "generational forgetting." In order to prevent a new drug crisis, HHS recommends an intensive education effort by schools, parents, and the news media.

The data suggest that Hispanics may be more susceptible to substance abuse than other ethnic groups. They have the highest rate of use of nearly all drugs in eighth grade, but not in twelfth. HHS theorizes that "their considerably higher dropout rate (compared to whites and blacks) may change their relative ranking by twelfth grade." Furthermore, even with the high dropout rate, Hispanic seniors have the highest usage rates of cocaine, crack, heroin, and steroids.

Many African American community leaders have long believed that whites are more likely to abuse drugs than blacks are. The data from HHS confirm this belief. Blacks have the lowest rate of substance abuse in all categories. Only 4 percent of black high school seniors smoke daily, compared with 21 percent of whites. Eleven percent of black twelfth graders admit to binge drinking, compared with 32 percent of whites. And, though most white Americans will swear that the opposite is true, young blacks have the lowest rate of illicit drug use of any ethnic group measured.

Community Approaches

Some researchers think that the success of anti-smoking programs is due in part to changing social norms, which have declared smoking unattractive. In contrast, the prevailing norm that drinking is acceptable and even desirable may be counteracting attempts to alter students' behavior. Drinking and substance abuse rates may not change much, researchers warn, until a larger social message gets across to young people.

It is just such a message that educators in Kansas City have tried to create through Project STAR, a two-year program combining a school-based curriculum with family and community components. The curriculum includes 12 sessions for seventh-graders that emphasize resistance skills, followed by five "booster" sessions in eighth grade. For homework, students interview their parents about family drug rules and techniques for avoiding drug abuse.

Project STAR staff, community leaders, and school administrators jointly plan the implementation of the school-based part of the program and coordinate it with other community prevention efforts. Project staff also give presentations to any group requesting information. Public knowledge of efforts in school is heightened by an active media campaign.

Evaluations show that Project STAR participants are less likely to abuse substances up to four years after the last booster session, although the magnitude of the effect is hardly dramatic. Mary Ann Pentz, director of community prevention research at the University of Southern California, conducted a six-year study following 7,500 Project STAR graduates and 7,500 controls from seventh through twelfth grade. Each year Pentz and her colleagues administered a survey and a biochemical smoking test to all 15,000 students. (Researchers have found that subjects are more likely to tell the truth if they know that even one aspect of behavior can be measured objectively. The smoking test should, by all accounts, increase the validity of the results in all areas.)

At the end of twelfth grade, the researchers found, participants showed a net reduction in heavy use of gateway drugs. Project STAR, like many other programs, was most successful in reducing tobacco use. The evaluation showed a net reduction of 12 percent in the number of "would-be daily smokers" among twelfth-graders. The corresponding decrease in the rates of monthly drunkenness and heavy marijuana use, however, was only 3 percent. A similar study of Project STAR participants in Indianapolis also found positive long-term effects, though of even smaller size.

Lessons from Drug Education

Perhaps the most fundamental lesson from the most recent round of drug and alcohol education programs is that the problem of substance abuse requires a variety of different and complementary approaches. Programs that affect student smoking do not significantly affect drinking and illegal drug use. And education that focuses on one of these problems may provide better results than programs that try to solve all of them.

Likewise, there is a difference between students experimenting with substances, those who have become chemically dependent, and those who have a history of chemical dependency in their families. To be effective, program planners will have to be clear about which substances and which populations they want to address.

In the evaluations of existing model programs, three features seem particularly associated with positive results:

- *Follow-up or booster sessions*. The RAND Corporation's 1993 study of 35,000 graduates of the Santa Monica, California, Project ALERT found that without consistent reinforcement, students appeared to forget what they had learned. According to the ten-year study, ALERT's social influence approach (similar to Project STAR's) persuaded many seventh- and eighth-graders to avoid marijuana and cigarettes, but not alcohol. Without the booster sessions, however, knowledge and anti-drug attitudes faded by tenth grade. The researchers urged "continued, strong reinforcement to resist drugs . . . during the high school years."

- *Peer teaching.* Adolescents are by definition turning away from adults and toward peers for guidance. Harnessing that developmental tendency can decrease destructive behavior. Tobler's 1992 survey of 91 drug-education programs identified the peer approach as a common denominator of successful programs. Indeed, according to a 1986 study of 143 programs, student-led education proved four times more effective than simply trying to increase students' self-esteem, and ten times more effective than teacher-delivered knowledge about drugs.

- *Community involvement.* The Kansas City program has achieved promising results by expanding drug education beyond the school building. While few such programs exist, community and school leaders are beginning to recognize the need for more coordinated approaches and particularly for enlisting the cooperation of parents.

For Further Information

P. Ellickson, R. Bell, and K. McGuigan. "Preventing Adolescent Drug Use: Long-Term Results of a Junior High Program." (Evaluation of Project ALERT.) *American Journal of Public Health* 83, no. 6 (June 1993): 856-861.

S. Ennett et al. "How Effective Is Drug Abuse Resistance Education? A Meta-Analysis of Project DARE Outcome Evaluations." *American Journal of Public Health* 84, no. 9 (September 1994): 1394-1401.

L. Johnston, P. O'Malley, and J. Bachman. *National Survey Results on Drug Use from Monitoring the Future Study, 1975-1992.* U.S. Department of Health and Human Services, 1993.

M. Pentz et al. "A Multicommunity Trial for Primary Prevention of Adolescent Drug Abuse: Effects on Drug Use Prevalence." (Evaluation of Project STAR.) *Journal of the American Medical Association* 261, no. 22 (June 9, 1989): 3259-3266.

Social Science Research and Evaluation, 121 Middlesex Turnpike, Burlington, MA 01803. Wayne Harding, director of operations.

N. Tobler. "Drug Prevention Programs Can Work: Research Findings." *Journal of Addictive Diseases* 11, no. 3 (1992): 1-28.

A Culture Obsessed With Thinness Pushes Some Adolescents into Eating Disorders

Susan Eaton

Soon after her usual midday meal of three ice-cream sandwiches, 15-year-old Ann would visit the school bathroom to brush her hair, gossip with friends, and vomit her lunch. After school, at soccer practice, Ann would sprint, jump rope, and scrimmage with teammates who marveled at her endurance. Later, she would jog to a supermarket, buy a loaf of bread, and devour it. Then she would go home and vomit again.

It took ten years before Ann even knew that her compulsive binge eating, exercising, and vomiting had a name: bulimia. Today, at age 30, she says she is able to control her bulimia but admits to "chronic dieting" and a preoccupation with her weight.

Eating disorders like bulimia and anorexia nervosa, as well as extreme dieting, are viewed primarily as psychological or health problems. But school nurses, nutrition educators, and teachers can help students at risk from these self-destructive behaviors if they also recognize them as cultural symptoms of a society obsessed with thinness.

In Search of Perfection

Little research on eating disorders has focused specifically on adolescents, but studies show that female athletes and dancers are among those at greatest risk. A 1990 NCAA survey found that 64 percent of college women athletes had some experience with an eating disorder. Academic high achievers and perfectionists also are at risk; a survey of female medical students found that 15 percent had suffered from eating disorders at some time. Many other students have a compulsive preoccupation with weight that can lead to unhealthy dieting and poor nutrition.

Clinical eating disorders are found mainly in women, though some researchers are now asking whether the problem is more common among men—especially wrestlers and certain other athletes—than has been generally assumed. Research is also beginning to challenge the widespread belief that these disorders are found only among white, upper-middle-class women.

A survey of 2,000 adolescent girls by the University of Michigan psychologist Adam Drenowski discovered that eating disorders were as common in low-income neighborhoods near Detroit as they were in the nearby wealthy suburbs. A recent survey in Florida found bulimia to be equally common in whites and blacks and *more* common at lower education and income levels.

Theories about the causes of eating disorders range from overinvolved parents to fear of intimacy. The best explanation experts can offer at present is that the condition probably results from a combination of psychological, social, and biological factors. But there is wide agreement that the behaviors can be at least partially explained by our society's preoccupation with thinness and the "perfect" female body.

These problems should be of particular concern to those who work with adolescents because of their characteristic striving to conform to an imagined "ideal" size, shape, or look. The normal increase in women's fat tissue that occurs in adolescence can cause distress and a longing to return to the thin, little-girl look so pervasive in advertising. One longitudinal study of 1,000 high school students found that more than 63 percent of ninth-grade girls and 70 percent of tenth- and twelfth-grade girls wanted to lose weight.

Severe clinical eating disorders are difficult to treat. Victims typically become adept at hiding the behavior; they may also genuinely believe that what they are doing is normal. Effective treatment often involves a combination of individual, group, and family therapy, coupled with antidepressant drugs. Teachers and coaches, meanwhile, can be most helpful by focusing on prevention and on creating an environment that does not exacerbate the problems.

Danger Signs

Anorexia nervosa is the rarest and most dangerous of these disorders. It usually begins in adolescence, but symptoms can develop as early as age nine. Anorectics simply stop eating. They may also exercise compulsively. Their images of their own bodies are distorted—that is, they see themselves as fat, even when they are in fact gaunt. Symptoms include constipation, anemia, brittle nails, dry skin, swollen joints, and loss of bone mass. Female victims who have reached puberty stop menstruating, and sexual development may be arrested.

The condition is dangerous because it can reduce heart rate and blood pressure to extremely low levels; the associated loss of potassium creates a risk of heart failure. Anorectics often fail to recognize their behavior as abnormal and therefore resist treatment.

Bulimia is more common than anorexia, but early research that reported an incidence as high as 35 percent among adolescent girls and young women has recently been challenged. Some new studies suggest that 5 percent to 10 percent of women may develop bulimia during their lives. Bulimic behavior includes bingeing—rapidly eating large amounts of food—and then "purging" by vomiting, by using diuretics or laxatives, or by fasting or exercising excessively. The clinical definition of the disorder is that the victim experiences two or more episodes of bingeing and purging each week for at least three months.

Bulimia is not as life-threatening as anorexia, but it can cause extreme fatigue, weakness, sore muscles, and bloating. The more serious consequences include dehydration, erosion of tooth enamel, rupture of the esophagus, and, in extreme cases, heart failure. Bulimia is harder to detect than anorexia because the victims go to extraordinary lengths to hide their behavior, and many bulimic girls and women maintain normal weight. Many women suffer from the two disorders simultaneously or sequentially.

People who are overly focused on dieting but whose behavior is not pathological may suffer from what some health educators and nutritionists call "chronic dieting syndrome." Again, the problem is found primarily among women. Chronic dieters may not experience the extreme turmoil and emotional distress associated with clinical eating disorders. But their lives are characterized by a constant concern with food intake and body shape. This preoccupation can drastically affect mood, self-esteem, and physical health.

Dieting is a way of life for these young women. They come to see hunger as something to be tolerated or ignored rather than satisfied. Unhealthy chronic dieting can include foolish schemes to lose weight, resulting in malnutrition and related health problems. Self-esteem also suffers from the continued failure to reduce one's body size to an impossible ideal.

Athletes at Risk

As women's sports gain parity with men's and more young women participate in competitive athletics it is becoming increasingly important for coaches to educate themselves about proper diet and nutrition for young athletes and to recognize the signs of eating disorders. These signs include weight loss, secretive behavior, petty stealing of money among teammates, swollen glands, and bloodshot eyes.

The athletes most at risk are those whose activities emphasize endurance, leanness, and aesthetic appeal, including ballet, gymnastics, figure skating, running, swimming, and competitive diving. Concern is growing about the "female athlete triad"—disordered eating, cessation of menstruation, and loss of bone mass and density. Sports such as wrestling and rowing, which require competitors to maintain a prescribed weight, can also precipitate eating disorders. Athletes may be particularly vulnerable to eating disorders when they face the challenge of moving to a more rigorous level of competition.

Experts advise coaches to keep watch, especially on perfectionists and overachievers. Research has shown a positive correlation between competitiveness and eating disorders. Coaches should encourage healthy, balanced eating and discourage dieting to "make weight" or to enhance performance. New team members should be advised that increased physical activity will probably require them to eat more to maintain their energy and stay healthy.

"Often it's the parents and coaches who foster eating disorders," says Dr. Alexandra Eliot, codirector of the Outpatient Eating Disorder Clinic at Children's Hospital in Boston. "Coaches need to speak about the danger of overexercising and must take the responsibility to say to some athletes, 'You are exercising too much.'"

What Teachers Can Do

For young adolescents who are influenced by the standards of physical beauty pervading television, films, magazines, and newspapers, a strictly medical pespective on eating and weight control may not be compelling. Girls and boys alike may not accept the medical definition of "appropriate" weight for their height and body type.

Teachers can, however, use scientific knowledge to help students critically examine the media images and societal standards that help precipitate disordered eating. For example, biological facts about how genetically determined body sizes and shapes differ among women can spur a critical examination of the students' own concepts of attractiveness. A teacher might start such a discussion by asking students what influenced their standards of beauty. Students may begin to see that their judgments are not independent, but rather are based almost solely on images sold to them by advertising.

It may also be effective to analyze media images of women and the subtle messages they send. Such lessons do not require a discussion of medical issues or eating disorders. Many advertisements, for example, associate being slim with finding love and having fun. The same associations are made with alcohol and tobacco use and with perfumes. Looking at the magazines aimed at the teen market, it is easy to see why many young people come to see getting thin as the answer to the confusion and struggle for acceptance and control they face as adolescents.

"We've really created a monster with this obsession with the perfect body," says Dr. Eliot. "The hallmark of adolescence is going with the flow. Kids are imbued with the idea, from TV and fashion magazines, that the perfect body is excessively thin."

Jeanne Gavrin, a Boston-area counselor and consultant, has developed slide shows for parents, teachers, and students to illustrate the cultural origins of eating disorders. The images trace the changing norms of female beauty from Rubens's nudes through the "flapper" fashions of the 1920s, Marilyn Monroe, the Barbie doll (with her disproportionately large breasts and tiny waist), Twiggy, and the "waif" look currently favored in fashion models.

"I also point out the magazine articles on dieting opposite ads and recipes for chocolate cake," says Gavrin. "The message—that you're supposed to get everything you want but still be thin—contributes to eating disorders."

Once students begin to understand advertisers' manipulation of their normal desires and anxieties, they may become more critical of the images that influence their feelings about their own worth and attractiveness. At the same time, teachers should not expect instant enlightenment, according to clinical psychologist Robert Kegan of Harvard: "It is incredibly difficult to get adolescents to distinguish their own real values from Madison Avenue internalizations. They can learn all about the propaganda and *still* tell you they've got to admit that thin looks good."

In spite of the difficulties, children and teens—like adults—need to get an alternative message: that thinness probably doesn't equal happiness or health. Educators, like coaches, should stress the virtues of a balanced life—one that is not marked by incessant competition or striving toward a distorted model of "perfection" of any type—academic, athletic, or aesthetic.

For Further Information

American Anorexia/Bulimia Assoc. 418 E. 76 St., New York, NY 10021.

Anorexia Bulimia Care. 545 Concord Ave., Cambridge, MA 02138; 617-492-7670.

N. Clark. *Nancy Clark's Sports Nutrition Guidebook*. Champaign, IL: Leisure Press, 1990.

J. Gavrin. Metro West Eating Disorders Awareness and Prevention. 617-894-8264.

R. A. Gordon. *Anorexia and Bulimia: Anatomy of a Social Epidemic*. Cambridge, MA: Blackwell, 1990.

National Association of Anorexia Nervosa and Associated Disorders. P.O. Box 7, Highland Park, IL 60035; 312-831-3438.

D. Taub. "Eating Disorders Among Adolescent Female Athletes." *Adolescence* 27, no. 108 (Winter 1992): 833.

Preventing Adolescent Suicide: Beyond Myths to a New Understanding

Helen Featherstone and Lisa Birk

Among adolescents, only motor vehicle accidents and homicide claim more lives than suicide. Suicide rates of 15- to 19-year-olds have been increasing steadily in recent years, nearly tripling since 1960. In 1991, the most recent year for which statistics are available, about 11 of every 100,000 teenagers took their own lives.

Teachers and counselors responded to this disturbing trend with workshops on "warning signs" and programs designed to prevent suicide in their schools. But despite the wide attention, frank discussions, a variety of programs, and genuine concern, fundamental questions about preventing suicide remain unanswered. Who is likely to attempt suicide? Do school-based programs reach and deter the young people who are most at risk? Can these programs actually push fragile adolescents toward suicide?

Individual Risk Factors

Accurately identifying individuals at risk of suicide is a tricky business. Common myths that portray suicide as an instant reaction to a stressful event obscure the reality. Almost all teens and adults who attempt or succeed at suicide have a long, painful history of depression and often aggression. The question is further complicated because many young people exhibit or experience one or more risk factors but never attempt suicide. Still, a list of typical circumstances, attributes, and behaviors may be useful in identifying—and perhaps inhibiting—potential suicides.

Using a method called psychological autopsy, David Shaffer and Madelyn Gould of Columbia University reconstruct profiles of adolescent suicides through extensive interviews with peers and relatives. They have uncovered these risk factors: depression, bipolar illness (also called manic-depressive illness), substance abuse, prior suicide attempts, a family history of suicidal behavior, and the availability of a gun.

Educators and medical professionals once thought "anxious" and "perfectionist" teenagers were at particular risk for suicide. Now, however, the most vulnerable group appears to be students with at least one psychiatric disorder such as depression, bipolar illness, or substance abuse. One 1988 study found that 25 of 27 cases of adolescent suicide involved at least one psychiatric disorder. Most young people who kill themselves have had longstanding, significant problems in school, with their families, and sometimes with the law.

Certain populations may be more prone to depression and therefore more inclined to suicide. A U.S. Department of Health and Human Services (HHS) study revealed that gay and lesbian youth account for about one-third of all teen suicides, and are two to three times more likely than their straight peers to attempt suicide (see "Gay Students Find Little Support in Most Schools," page 115). Native Americans kill themselves at ten times the rate of whites. (Black Americans, however, are significantly less likely than whites to commit suicide across all age groups.) A 1988 survey of 129 high schools indicated that students with learning disabilities accounted for 14 percent of all suicide-related incidents, though the proportion of students overall with identified learning disabilities rarely exceeds 5 percent.

Boys kill themselves at a rate nearly six times higher than girls. In 1991, approximately 18 young men out of every 100,000 between age 15 and 19 committed suicide. The rate for young women was about 3 per 100,000.

The gender difference has given rise to several possible explanations. Young white women are more inclined to call hotlines, and may therefore receive crisis intervention or even long-term help that reduces the suicidal impulse. Also, those who choose firearms rather than pills or other methods are more likely to die—and males choose guns more often than females.

Suicide experts debate the meaning of method. Are those who choose guns more serious, while those who choose less violent means, such as pills, merely "asking for help"? Some researchers propose a continuum model, observing that a person is unlikely to die by his own hand without first having imagined, planned, and attempted suicide before. Others note the demographic differences between those who die and those who survive and see gradations in seriousness of intent. Both conclusions, however, come from studies of a skewed sample population: young people referred to psychiatric clinics. A broader sample might yield different results.

Anthony Adcock of Troy State University in Alabama theorizes that drinking too much, acting out, and getting into trouble may be attempts to forestall depression. His 1991 study found that both male and female adolescents who drink and are sexually active are at greater risk for suicide than their peers.

The myth that suicide is a response to a single traumatic event may be perpetuated by the fact that a stressful event often triggers a suicidal incident, but only after a long history of depression and acting out. A breakup with a girlfriend or boyfriend, an argument with parents, or any event that causes feelings of rejection, humiliation, futility, or anger is a common precursor to suicide. Being the victim of sexual or other physical assault seems to be a particularly important risk factor for girls.

Friends and family of the victim may—unintentionally—contribute to the false stereotyping of suicides. Powerful forces lead the grieving to gloss over the darker side of the victim's life: it is "wrong" to speak ill of the dead; it is embarrassing to have "missed the signs" of impending tragedy; and it is painful to acknowledge the problems in our lives. A best friend may describe the dead boy as captain of the football team, but leave out the 36 days he skipped school. A father may describe his daughter's smile on prom night, but leave out the nights he smelled alcohol on her breath. The news media often contribute to the false image. The more "newsworthy" suicides are the shocking cases of smart, popular kids who killed themselves anyway.

The Contagion Factor

When the worst happens, many adults worry about copycat suicides among young people. Dramatic news coverage of a suicide and even educational programs that present compelling details do appear to run the risk of glorifying suicide and provoking other attempts. The *New England Journal of Medicine* has published two studies showing that TV presentations of suicide—both factual accounts and fictional dramas—preceded a temporary, otherwise inexplicable rise in the number of self-inflicted deaths.

In one of these studies, Madelyn Gould looked at the impact of four television dramas on teen suicide rates in the New York City area. She found that TV was a trigger factor, but that the shows in themselves "are not going to take healthy kids and cause them to kill themselves." Gould warns, however, that "there are some other kids out there—disturbed kids, troubled kids—who see these programs at a vulnerable time. That's not to say they would have been healthy otherwise or that they would have had good lives. But they might not have killed themselves."

The producers of the four shows had hoped to teach the public about suicide prevention. They consulted experts as they planned the programs and made additional educational materials available through local television stations. "There were educational and preventive elements in those made-for-TV movies," says David Clark, executive director of the Center for Suicide Research and Prevention at Chicago's Rush–Presbyterian–St. Luke's Medical Center. "There were also provocative elements—when the story is highly dramatic, for instance, or the heroine is Molly Ringwald and she's so attractive and the kids have seen her starring in another movie the month before."

The research of David Phillips and Lundie Carstensen of the University of California at San Diego supports this point of view. Looking at national television news coverage of 38 suicides over seven years, they found that news and feature stories of these deaths were consistently followed by a surge of suicide attempts among teens.

Combatting suicide contagion may be as simple as changing the presentation of facts surrounding a suicide. In 1994, the Centers for Disease Control (CDC) recommended that "certain characteristics of news coverage, rather than news coverage itself, should be avoided." To minimize the likelihood of suicide imitation, the CDC called for "concise and factual" reporting that limits or avoids dramatic photographs, "how-to" descriptions of suicide, and oversimplified explanations of the causes—such as the fact that the victim had recently had a fight with his parents. The Centers also recommended that communities avoid glorifying the deceased. Specifically, the CDC suggests reducing or eliminating public eulogies, flags flying at half-mast, and erecting permanent public memorials. "Susceptible persons [may believe] that society is honoring the suicidal behavior of the deceased person, rather than mourning the person's death," concludes the report.

High school principal Sidney Barish in Port Washington, New York, found the matter-of-fact approach useful when confronted with a student's suicide. He persuaded both the local newspaper and the school paper to print the obituary and leave out the text of the student's suicide letter. "This was not an issue about freedom of the press," Barish wrote in the *NASSP Bulletin*. "It was a matter of life and death."

Helping Those at Risk

Many schools are taking an aggressive approach, choosing among some 400 suicide prevention curricula. One program takes students to visit a morgue, applying the theory that young people court death because they can't imagine mortality. But most programs are two hours long and include statistics about adolescent suicide, a list of warning signs, a list of resources, and a discussion of problem-solving skills and stress-reduction techniques. Most de-emphasize mental illness in a well-intentioned attempt to destigmatize suicide and thus increase help-seeking behaviors. Instead, they incorrectly portray suicide as a reaction to normal adolescent problems—an approach that may backfire.

Ann Garland and Edward Zigler of Yale University speculate that destigmatizing suicide "may normalize the behavior and reduce potentially protective taboos." One well-controlled study with a sample size of 1,000 and a control group of equal size revealed that participation in a suicide prevention program resulted in a small but significant increase in the number of students who believed suicide could be a solution to problems. The number of actual suicide attempts, however, remained unchanged.

Some question the efficacy of school-based suicide prevention programs because those most at risk may be absent. A 1986 study found that many suicide victims were absent from school before killing themselves. Two 1989 studies found runaways, dropouts, and incarcerated youths to have high suicide rates. Clearly, prevention programs held in school can do little for those who are elsewhere.

Other researchers raise a more fundamental question. Can we know which programs work? Most assessments of suicide prevention programs base their conclusions on self-reporting of attitudes and beliefs rather than measurable behaviors. "Nobody has the foggiest idea about how one program works compared to the next," warns David Clark. "Everyone swears their program works and they'll point to four or five kids they brought back from the edge—but nobody knows whether there are any casualties or kids made worse, whether suicide rates in the general area go down afterward, or whether two or three years later the program has left anything in the school."

Despite the data gaps, recent research can point educators in the right direction. Because teenagers at risk tend to have multiple problems, from school failures and family problems to alcohol abuse and depression, the best prevention program is the one that addresses the widest spectrum of needs. Some teen suicides might be prevented by treating alcoholism and abuse of other substances that depress mood and diminish judgment. Limiting the availability of guns may also help. Because a large number of young people consider suicide at some time and try unsuccessfully to kill themselves, Jeffrey Boyd and Eve Mosicki of the National Institute of Mental Health believe that the wide availability of guns increases the chances that adolescents with a passing impulse toward suicide will end up dead.

Students are receptive to mental health programs. General health and prevention programs offering information about a variety of problems could be used to help students identify peers in distress. Many researchers suggest identifying, tracking, and counseling suicide-prone students—remembering that those who act out may be most in danger. Several studies conclude that youth are leery of seeking adult help, but will, when asked, reveal suicidal thoughts and emotional problems. A targeted intervention may succeed where generalized programs have failed.

If the worst should occur and a student attempts or actually commits suicide, talk with mental health professionals about how to respond. Both adults and adolescents will have to deal with their own grief, anger, and confusion. Locate resources and figure out how to avoid sensationalizing and glamorizing the death.

For Further Information

A. Adcock, S. Nagy, and J. Simpson. "Selected Risk Factors in Adolescent Suicide Attempts." *Adolescence* 26, no. 104 (Winter 1991): 817-828.
American Association of Suicidology, 2459 S. Ash St., Denver, CO 80222.

S. Barish. "Responding to Adolescent Suicide." *NASSP Bulletin* 75, no. 538 (November 1991): 98-103.

A. Garland and E. Zigler. "Adolescent Suicide Prevention: Current Research and Social Policy Implications." *American Psychologist* 48, no. 2 (February 1993): 169-182.

D. Huntington and W. Bender. "Adolescents with Learning Disabilities at Risk? Emotional Well-Being, Depression, and Suicide." *Journal of Learning Disabilities* 26, no. 3 (March 1993): 159-166.

P. O'Carroll and L. Potter. "Suicide Contagion and the Reporting of Suicide: Recommendations from a National Workshop." *Morbidity and Mortality Weekly Report* 43, no. RR-6 (April 22, 1994): 13-18.

D. Phillips and L. Carstensen. "Clustering of Teenage Suicides After Television News Stories About Suicide." *New England Journal of Medicine* 315, no. 11 (September 1986): 685-689.

Suicide Digest. Published quarterly by the Center for Suicide Research and Prevention, Rush-Presbyterian-St. Luke's Medical Center, 1720 W. Polk St., Chicago, IL 60612.

Part III:
Strategies
For Preventing
Violence

The Killing Grounds: Can Schools Help Stem The Violence?

Adria Steinberg

In 1991, the chance that a white male between the ages of 15 and 19 would die from a gunshot surpassed his chance of dying from natural causes. In 1988, nearly half of all deaths among black male teens were by firearms. The United States, according to a recent Senate Judiciary Committee report, is the most violent and self-destructive nation in the industrialized world.

Most reports of teen violence emerge from urban areas where many children grow up surrounded by what child advocates aptly call "the violence of poverty." But young people in rural and suburban areas are not immune to the epidemic of violence.

While reliable statistics are hard to compile, there is evidence that date rape and domestic abuse cross lines of social class and race, and that patterns of violence begin long before adolescence. Certainly children everywhere must learn to deal with schoolyard and neighborhood bullies.

And, of course, television reaches into every home with its steady diet of murder and mayhem. Violence is marketed directly to children in the form of cartoons, many of which serve as extended advertisements for "action figures" fully outfitted with arsenals of weapons. Teachers and parents in all kinds of communities watch children's play with growing concern about the preoccupation with violence.

Despite such concern, there is little consensus on what schools can or should do, beyond ensuring safety within the school building. Nevertheless, promising experiments have begun to emerge—from special intervention programs for weapon-toting teenagers to broad-based classroom and even school-wide prevention programs that teach students to resolve conflicts peacefully and help them develop into caring, altruistic adults.

Friends Fight

Deborah Prothrow-Stith of the Harvard University School of Public Health tells a story from her early days as an intern. While she sutured a scalp wound of a teenager who had signed himself into the emergency room, he told her not to plan on getting any rest that evening, because "the person who did this to me is going to be in the ER in about an hour—and you're going to get all the practice you need."

At the time, such blatant warnings went without response. The underlying assumption was that a victim of violence had simply been unlucky enough to get in the way of the wrong person. "It was thought that certain individuals would randomly behave aggressively toward anyone," notes Ron Slaby of Harvard University.

Today the boy's message would be taken seriously, because it is now understood that violence often erupts in the context of peer relationships. Students who witness or are victims of violence typically know the assailant and sometimes even participate in the instigation or maintenance of the conflict. The same young person may, at different times, play the roles of perpetrator, victim, and bystander.

Not a Wimp

One way to get a handle on the perplexing nature of violence among adolescents is to understand the attitudes and beliefs that support the development of aggression. Researchers have found a number of important differences in the way aggressive and unaggressive youth think about violence.

In a study Slaby conducted with Nancy Guerra, students were given vignettes describing somewhat ambiguous situations of potential conflict. They compared the responses of three groups of teens: adolescents who had been incarcerated for violent offenses, students nominated by teachers and other students as "high aggressive," and students nominated as "low aggressive."

Drawing from this study and from earlier studies of younger boys conducted by Kenneth Dodge and Cynthia Frame of Indiana University, Slaby and Guerra have come up with a list of "cognitive mediators"—habits of thinking and sets of beliefs—that appear to be associated with the use of violence. Aggressive youth, they note, tend to attribute hostility to others, search for few facts in trying to understand a situation, and have difficulty envisioning alternative solutions, especially nonviolent ones.

The juvenile offenders, even though they have the most experience with violence, seem to have the least sense of its harmful consequences. They are likely to consider violence a legitimate response, and maybe even a necessary one to avoid being thought of as a wimp or a patsy. They also tend to ignore or deny the suffering of the victim.

Such findings raise questions about the currently popular notion that making young people feel better about themselves will reduce violence. Aggressive students, Slaby explains, may actually connect their self-esteem to their ability to bully others. Joining a gang can in itself be a boost to self-esteem, unless kids change how they think and what they believe about violence and develop alternative, nonviolent means for gaining what they need and want.

Get the Word Out

School people concerned about the escalating violence can now choose among a growing number of prevention curricula. Only some of these are based on new understandings about aggression, cautions Slaby, who heads a project at Education Development Center (EDC) in Newton, Massachusetts, that publishes a curriculum for middle schools.

At the high school level, EDC's Health and Human Development Program distributes a curriculum developed by Prothrow-Stith. The focus of the ten-session course is on helping adolescents understand and control their anger through learning and practicing conflict resolution.

The curriculum is part of a larger Violence Prevention Project, which Prothrow-Stith launched in 1987 with the goal of creating "a new community ethos supportive of violence prevention." Using a public health strategy, the project attempts to involve everyone who is in contact with youth—from pediatricians to coaches—in reinforcing the message that it does not make sense to "fight it out."

Surprisingly, this is not the message that adults typically give to kids. While adults certainly do not want teenagers to shoot each other, many will tell kids to "fight back—don't be a wimp" in response to a playground incident. "We realized," Prothrow-Stith notes, "that we needed to offer more training to the adults, that we had to change their attitudes before we could change the kids." She sees this as one of the most valuable lessons from the first five years of the Violence Prevention Project. Recent evaluations of the program point to another lesson: prevention curricula by themselves are unlikely to have any effect (see page 73).

Start Early

Educators are also learning that prevention efforts need to begin early. Kids do not just "grow out" of being bullies or perpetual victims. "Interpersonal relationships in school are a predictor of both present and future personal adjustment," says Robert Selman of Harvard University.

While teachers are aware of the importance of early relationships, many are not sure what to do when faced with conflict. Until recently, for example, it was not uncommon for adults to encourage young children to vent their anger on a punching bag or to beat up a pillow. Such advice is based on the notion that aggression generates spontaneously and builds up inside children, who must then vent some of it to avoid a more harmful explosion later.

Today, experts on conflict resolution take a different view. While the capacity for violence may be inborn, children learn to be aggressive. Punching a pillow may bring momentary relief, but does not expose the child to new, nonviolent models for dealing with anger or aggression.

Who Wins?

Nancy Carlsson-Paige and Diane Levin, the authors of *The War Play Dilemma,* point out that even 5- and 6-year-olds can understand many of the elements of arriving at "win-win" solutions. What is needed is a teacher who understands how to nurture the growth of these skills in developmentally appropriate ways.

"He hit me." "She took the paddle." In their research in primary-grade classrooms, Carlsson-Paige and Levin hear many such examples of the way children define a problem that has erupted between them. Rather than simply telling the children to take turns with the desired object, or putting it away, the teacher can redefine the situation as a shared problem. For example, the teacher might say, "You both want the paddle; there's only one."

In this way the teacher can help young children understand the problem in concrete, physical terms that make sense to them. It is the first step in working toward a positive solution and in helping the children learn to use such terms to talk about their problems among themselves.

Similarly, the teacher can model and reinforce other parts of the problem-solving process—helping students to notice how specific actions contributed to the problem, to negotiate with one another, and to generate and evaluate a variety of possible solutions. "Children develop an understanding of conflict and how to resolve it through a long slow process of construction," the researchers conclude.

What Teachers Need

"I've been teaching for twenty years, and every year it gets worse and worse. There's more fighting. The kids seem to have such short fuses—the least little thing sets them off. They see violence on the street and at home, and they don't know any other ways to deal with conflict."

Concerns about escalating violence have led some elementary schools—like the one this teacher works in—to seek help. Her school participates in a conflict-resolution program developed by William Kreidler of Educators for Social Responsibility.

"As a young teacher," Kreidler explains, "I wanted to stop all conflict in my classroom. But then I realized that wasn't possible or desirable, and that I could use conflict as a learning tool." As children become skilled peacemakers, the classroom becomes a more productive environment. And when conflicts do erupt, children and teachers gain valuable practice in solving social problems.

Kreidler's program includes twenty hours of training for teachers (K-6), followed by ten hours of in-class support. This kind of commitment of time is necessary, he notes, because there is much more involved than simply giving teachers a chance to learn and practice new skills in conflict resolution. Like Prothrow-Smith, Kreidler believes that adults need to reconsider their own views on conflict.

For example, during the training teachers take a new look at their approaches to classroom management—the way they structure the classroom and develop and enforce rules. They look at what it might mean to create a classroom and school environment in which kids would want to resolve things peacefully.

Teachers also look at the curriculum, to see how they can weave conflict resolution into their social studies, reading, and math lessons. Although it is possible to teach conflict-resolution skills in isolation, it is clearly preferable to connect these skills to the overall curriculum and social climate of the classroom and the school. Kreidler draws a portrait of a "peaceable classroom," characterized by cooperation, appreciation for diversity, and sensitivity to emotions and varying perspectives.

It Works

"It's a wonderful thing to see: these kids are helping each other, caring for each other. I said to myself, 'Holy mackerel! Don't tell me this actually works!'"

Phil Wallace taught fourth grade in a San Ramon Valley, California, school participating in the Child Development Project (CDP). Now retired, he occasionally serves as a substitute teacher in the junior high, where he has noticed "a tremendous difference" between children who come from CDP and non-CDP schools.

The CDP is now in its second decade, expanding to new districts after a seven-year study of the project found evidence that schools can help children become more caring and responsible. "The CDP is the first long-term, comprehensive, school-based project in prosocial education," says Alfie Kohn, who quotes Wallace and features the CDP in his book, *The Brighter Side of Human Nature: Altruism and Empathy in Everyday Life.*

Teachers in CDP schools receive training in an innovative approach to classroom management and discipline—one that rejects traditional carrot-and-stick strategies. Starting in kindergarten, children and teachers decide together how to organize the classroom and how to handle behavior problems so as to reinforce values like caring and helping others.

Prosocial values are embedded in what is taught. The books and stories children read focus on characters facing moral issues, such as how to maintain their own values in the face of peer pressure. How classes are taught is also important. Students spend part of each day in cooperative learning groups, solving problems together.

The cooperative spirit goes beyond the classroom and into the home, where children find out what their parents think about some of the stories and issues discussed in school. The program also gives kids a chance to serve as models themselves, through a buddy program that pairs older and younger children for school outings or tutoring. Finally, students take their caring out into the community by participating in service projects.

While the separate elements of the CDP approach are not, as one teacher put it, "foreign or shocking or new," the combination represents a very different way of educating young people. In the words of a San Ramon city council member, "It's difficult to argue with constructive, positive influences that bring results."

A longitudinal comparison between students participating in the program and those in non-CDP schools turned up significant differences. For example, CDP children engaged in more spontaneous prosocial behaviors in class, understood hypothetical conflict situations better, and were more likely to take everyone's needs into account in dealing with such situations.

At the same time, these children considered it important to be assertive about their own beliefs. Teaching kids to be caring does not mean turning them into doormats, according to Eric Schaps, the director of CDP. In an interview with Kohn he explains: "We're looking for a healthy balance of concern for self and concern for others."

Furthermore, the long-term study alleviated teachers' fears that emphasizing values in the classroom might cut down on academic learning. Children in CDP schools received scores on standardized tests comparable to those of their peers in other schools. And, when the original cohort of kids reached sixth grade, their essays were evaluated more positively (in a blind rating system) than those written by non-CDP peers.

In 1988 these positive results led to an expansion of the program to Hayward, a neighboring school district with a more ethnically heterogeneous population. By the fall of 1991, six other districts, five of them urban, were participating.

It is too early to tell how well the project will transfer. Schaps points to two critical preconditions for success: intensive teacher training and support from the principal. "We expect to adapt what we are doing," adds program director Marilyn Watson, "especially in communities where families are experiencing great stress." She points to the work of James Comer, whose School Development Project in New Haven, Connecticut, is a model of how schools and low-income parents can work together to enhance the social development of children.

"The attitude of many people," says Kohn, "is that once you get kids well-behaved, that's where the responsibility ends." In his view, the CDP has already made an important contribution to challenging that attitude by demonstrating "that children can be raised to work with, care for, and help each other, and that schools can play a major role in that process."

For Further Information

N. Carlsson-Paige and D. E. Levin. "Making Peace in Violent Times: A Constructivist Approach to Conflict Resolution." *Young Children* 48, no. 1 (November 1992): 4-13.

N. Carlsson-Paige and D. E. Levin. *The War Play Dilemma.* New York: Teachers College Press, 1987.

Child Development Project, Developmental Studies Center, 2000 Embarcadero, Oakland, CA 94606; 510-533-0213.

K. A. Dodge and C. L. Frame. "Social Cognitive Biases and Deficits in Aggressive Boys." *Child Development* 53, no. 3 (1982): 620-635.

N. G. Guerra and R. G. Slaby. "Cognitive Mediators of Aggression in Adolescent Offenders: 2. Intervention." *Developmental Psychology* 26, no. 2 (March 1990): 269-277.

A. Kohn. "The ABC's of Caring." *Teacher Magazine* (January 1990).

A. Kohn. *The Brighter Side of Human Nature: Altruism and Empathy in Everyday Life.* New York: Basic Books, 1990.

W. J. Kreidler. *Creative Conflict Resolution: More Than 200 Activities for Keeping Peace in the Classroom, K-6.* Glenview, IL: Scott, Foresman, 1984.

W. J. Kreidler. *Elementary Perspectives #1: Teaching Concepts of Peace and Conflict.* Boston: Educators for Social Responsibility, 1990.

National Association for Mediation in Education. "Violence Prevention in Our Schools." *The Fourth R: Newsletter of the NAME* 28 (August/September 1990).

D. Prothrow-Stith, H. Spivak, and A. J. Hausman. "The Violence Prevention Project: A Public Health Approach." *Science, Technology and Human Values* 12, nos. 3 and 4 (Summer/Fall 1987): 67-69.

D. Prothrow-Stith, M.D., with M. Weissman. *Deadly Consequences.* New York: HarperCollins, 1991.

R. L. Selman and M. Glidden. "Negotiation Strategies for Youth." *School Safety* 18 (Fall 1987): 18-21.

R. G. Slaby and N. G. Guerra. "Cognitive Mediators of Aggression in Adolescent Offenders: 1. Assessment." *Developmental Psychology* 24, no. 4 (1988): 580-588.

D. Solomon, M. S. Watson, K. L. Delucchi, E. Schaps, and V. Battistich. "Enhancing Children's Prosocial Behavior in the Classroom." *American Educational Research Journal* 25, no. 4 (1988): 527-554.

Research Raises Troubling Questions About Violence Prevention Programs

Marc Posner

It's every principal's nightmare. The sound of gunshots. The phone call imploring you to rush to the cafeteria where an argument that began on the street has exploded. And when the ambulance and the police have gone there will be television cameras, microphones, and reporters' questions, a deluge of phone calls from frightened parents, and an emergency school board meeting. The question you will hear over and over is "What are you going to do to make sure this does not happen again?"

An increasing number of public and private school administrators face situations involving serious violence perpetrated by and against adolescents. School officials are responding by adding violence prevention programs—often a commercially available "off-the-shelf" package—to their schools' already overcrowded curricula. But few administrators under pressure to "do something" about violence have the resources or the expertise to assess the extent of their school's violence problem, to judge whether the program they have chosen is appropriate for their students, or to find evidence that the program actually works. In fact, researchers are beginning to question whether the most commonly used school-based programs for violence prevention and conflict resolution actually do what they are supposed to do.

More Harm Than Good?

Most evaluations of these programs reveal little evidence of success. Daniel Webster of the Injury Prevention Center at Johns Hopkins University reviewed evaluations of three widely used curricula—the Violence Prevention Curriculum for Adolescents by Deborah Prothrow-Stith, the Washington (DC) Community Violence Prevention Program, and Positive Adolescent Choices Training—and found "no evidence that such programs produce long-term changes in violent behavior or risk of victimization." Indeed, Webster argues that the main function of these programs is to provide "political cover" for school officials and politicians, and that they may do more harm than good by distracting the public from the real causes of youth violence.

A survey of 51 programs by Renee Wilson-Brewer and colleagues at Education Development Center (EDC) in Newton, Massachusetts, found that fewer than half even claimed to have reduced levels of violence. Most claimed to have had effects that program staff members assumed would help prevent violence, such as creating community awareness or having a substantial number of students complete the program, but few had any data to back up their assumptions.

Nancy Guerra and Patrick Tolan of the University of Illinois reviewed the existing research and identified some promising strategies warranting further study, but concluded that "well-intentioned efforts are being applied to many children and adolescents without indication of their effects. . . . Not only have programs that have been earnestly launched been ineffective, but some of our seemingly best ideas have led to worsening the behavior of those subjected to the intervention." This disturbing negative effect, Guerra explains, results from the difficulty of identifying high-risk students. Kids who are wrongly placed in targeted violence prevention programs (which, ironically, seem to have the greatest impact) may become more violence-prone than if they had not been exposed to the programs.

Defenders of the programs blame the lack of evidence of their success on the shortcomings of the evaluations. It is true that few programs have the resources and expertise necessary for evaluating behavioral outcomes and for long-term follow-up. Most evaluations lack adequate sample sizes, matched comparison groups, and objective measures of behavioral outcomes. Many use tests of student attitudes or self-reported behavior that measure little but the students' ability to give the answers expected of them.

Evaluations based on teachers' classroom observations are equally suspect. Guerra warns that "testimonials should not be confused with evaluations." Well-meaning teachers may "see" a reduction in violence among students where none exists. Or, driven by honest concern and media attention, they may exaggerate the levels of violence that existed before their intervention. Evaluations based on "objective" behavioral outcomes like discipline and arrest records are at the mercy of the inconsistencies of school discipline policies and the juvenile justice system.

Flaws in the Design

Researchers are beginning to suspect that the lack of evidence for success in violence prevention is not just because of inadequate evaluation efforts. Many programs have serious flaws that make them highly unlikely to overcome the inherent difficulties of changing complex human behavior. Too often, they lump together a broad range of behaviors and people, ignoring the fact that different types of people turn to violence for very different reasons.

Few school-based prevention programs target the relatively small group of young people who commit acts of serious violence. Daniel Webster points out that many conflict resolution programs teach the kinds of negotiation skills that may be useful for middle-class students whose disputes stem from competing interests, but not for poor, high-risk youth for whom violent conflict is often a result of macho posturing and competition for status. Nancy Guerra similarly criticizes the notion that a program reflecting middle-class norms will affect the behavior of all violent youth. "A sixteen-year-old who sticks up a McDonald's," she notes, "does not have a conflict with the person behind the cash register."

The field of violence prevention faces an even greater challenge than learning how to target its programs: the inherent difficulty of creating and implementing any school-based program that actually changes behavior. Alcohol- and drug-abuse prevention efforts have been subjected to more research, better evaluation, and wider and more consistent implementation than violence prevention programs, yet serious questions remain about the effectiveness of many widely used programs.

This is not to say that alcohol- and drug-abuse prevention efforts never work. Nancy Tobler of the State University of New York examined the evaluations of almost 150 programs and found some that were effective. But the key to success, she says, is knowing "which types of programs should be offered to whom, by whom, and at what age." Programs must take into account the age group being targeted, the drugs being targeted, the selection and training of leaders, and the influence of the community. Many alcohol and drug programs, and most violence prevention programs, ignore these critical variables.

Violence often results from a complex interaction of environmental, social, and psychological factors such as the learned behavior of responding to conflict with violence, the effects of drugs or alcohol, the presence of weapons, the absence of positive family relationships and adult supervision. Few violence prevention programs can muster the resources to affect all the possible causes.

Behavioral skills learned in school health classes and substance-abuse prevention programs generally suffer a marked decline after six months. The key to providing students with the skills, knowledge, and motivation they require to become healthy adults is a comprehensive program that responds to the new risks and pressures that arise with each developmental stage. The onset of puberty, the increased presence of alcohol, drugs, and weapons in a young person's environment, and growing economic pressures all increase the risk of being a perpetrator or a victim of violence. A violence prevention program that takes place over a couple of weeks at one grade level has little hope of success. Addressing these risks requires a sustained effort over the child's entire school career.

Promising Strategies

Educators have neither the resources nor the responsibility to change all the social factors that impel young people toward violence. But they do have the power to make some changes in their schools. Children at high risk of violence, academic failure, drug abuse, and dropping out often lack a connection to any positive social entity—family, peer group, or church. Guerra and Tolan found that many of the most promising strategies were family interventions that taught parenting skills and improved family relationships. They also found evidence to suggest that effective school-based programs should focus not just on students but on the school itself as well.

Schools that provide a positive social attachment for youth can, at least in part, lessen the estrangement and hopelessness that lead kids to the alternative culture of gangs. Daniel Webster suggests assigning teams of teachers to follow cohorts of students through several grades, instead of changing teachers every year. This, he argues, can create more positive and lasting bonds between students and their school. Webster also suggests keeping schools open for supervised extracurricular activities on afternoons, evenings, and weekends, and during the summer. Keeping students away from the streets, gangs, drugs, and boredom for even a few hours after classes will at least diminish the amount of time that the negative influences have to do their work. At the same time, there is no hard evidence from evaluations that such strategies actually work better than others.

Schools may also have a part to play in protecting students from risks they encounter outside the classroom. Some researchers have attributed the dramatic increase in serious violence among youth to two intersecting trends: a large increase in the population of young men (the group that commits most violent crimes) and the unprecedented availability and acceptability of guns—especially semi-automatic handguns. The presence of a gun can lead to violence in situations where the presence of a different weapon, even a knife, will not. Obviously, a bullet fired in anger can cause more injury than a punch or slap.

Increased attention is being focused on school-based programs to steer youth away from carrying guns and associating with those who do. While there is no good evidence as yet about how well such programs work, the fact that they require less of a behavioral change on the part of students than some other approaches may be cause for optimism. On the other hand, these gun programs cannot be thought of as a substitute for what has become an almost universally accepted maxim in the public health community—that the most effective intervention for serious violence would be to outlaw the possession, manufacture, and sale of these weapons.

Television, movies, rap music, and video games are frequently criticized for their violent content and its presumed ill effects on young people. Much of this criticism is simplistic and ignores the more complex causes of violence. Still, the research on violence and the media (including that on sexual violence and pornography) indicates that a consistent depiction of violence as an acceptable method of resolving conflicts or increasing status and self-esteem contributes to the forces that impel so many youths toward this behavior. Critical viewing and media literacy programs that teach children how to interpret what they see and hear may be of some help.

Let the Buyer Beware

While violence prevention programs are not *the* solution, carefully designed, targeted, and implemented programs with good teacher training and technical support may be part of the solution. The Tolan-Guerra and EDC reviews suggest that strategies including cognitive mediation programs (in which young people are taught to change those habits of thought that lead them to respond violently to conflict) have shown some success in changing behavior. Webster, however, questions the potential of classroom interventions for changing habits acquired much earlier in life.

Whatever the merits of school-based violence prevention programs, there is no value in implementing the wrong program for the wrong reasons. Administrators should carefully assess their needs before adopting any program. Nancy Guerra reminds school officials that "one incident does not make a problem." One student caught with a gun does not necessarily mean your school needs metal detectors. If half the students are packing weapons, however, metal detectors can help provide a more secure environment.

Guerra also warns administrators to be careful consumers and not just grab the first program that comes across their desks. In many cases, she says, "whatever program has the glossiest cover and the best marketing plan gets implemented." She points out that ineffective programs can be dangerous if administrators and parents are lulled into thinking they are addressing the problem when they are not. Informed choices and effective strategies require input from parents, teachers, law enforcement agencies, and medical, public health, and social service personnel.

A good model at the state level is Illinois, which has amended its School Code to require districts to provide violence prevention or conflict resolution education in grades 4 through 12. As part of the effort, the Illinois Council for the Prevention of Violence has established a curriculum task force including representatives of a wide range of state and local groups. The task force is creating a framework for reviewing violence prevention curricula, identifying gaps, and making recommendations for the use of such curricula in Illinois schools. It will also pilot violence prevention programs in five districts to determine what kinds of technical assistance and other resources are most helpful.

The Power of Social Decay

We must also be realistic about the strength of the social forces that impel children towards violence. Even long-term educational interventions are not sufficient for children in neighborhoods whose economies and social structures are in ruins. Thus school health programs are increasingly being supplemented by breakfast and lunch programs and school-based health services. Violence prevention may prove most effective when it is one of a number of services offered as part of a "full-service school."

But violence is not like malnutrition or infectious diseases. Immunization in a school clinic can protect a child from measles. A good school breakfast and lunch can help make up for the lack of any dinner. But a ten-session violence prevention course cannot overcome the deprivations of a life of poverty or the pressures toward violence in the world outside school.

The burden of preventing violence cannot lie solely, or even primarily, on the shoulders of educators. Webster points out that many violence prevention programs assume there is "something wrong with the kids" that we can fix with educational intervention. A truer understanding of what is really wrong can be found in President Lyndon Johnson's address to the nation in July 1967, in the wake of a wave of urban violence:

"The only genuine, long-range solution for what has happened lies in an attack—mounted at every level—upon the conditions that breed despair and violence. All of us know what those conditions are: ignorance, discrimination, slums, poverty, disease, not enough jobs. We should attack these conditions—not because we are frightened by conflict, but because we are fired by conscience. We should attack them because there is simply no other way to achieve a decent and orderly society in America."

For Further Information

S. Cohen and R. Wilson-Brewer. *Violence Prevention for Young Adolescents: The State of the Art of Program Evaluation.* Available from the ERIC Clearinghouse (ED356441); 800-443-3742.

Options. A quarterly newsletter available from the CSN Adolescent Violence Prevention Resource Center, Education Development Center, 55 Chapel Street, Newton, MA 02158-1060. 617-969-7100.

A. Reiss and J. Roth, eds. *Understanding and Preventing Violence.* Washington, DC: National Academy Press, 1993.

R. Slaby et al. *Early Violence Prevention: Tools for Teachers of Young Children.* Washington, DC: National Association for the Education of Young Children, 1995.

N. Tobler. "Drug Prevention Programs That Can Work: Research Findings." *Journal of Addictive Diseases* 11, no. 3 (1992): 1-28.

P. Tolan and N. Guerra. *What Works in Reducing Adolescent Violence: An Empirical Review of the Field.* Denver: Center for the Study of Prevention of Violence, University of Colorado, in press.

Violence Prevention News. Illinois Council for the Prevention of Violence, 123 S. Seventh Street, Suite 500, Springfield, IL 62701.

D. Webster. "The Unconvincing Case for School-Based Conflict Resolution Programs for Adolescents." *Health Affairs* 12, no. 4 (Winter 1993): 126-140.

R. Wilson-Brewer, S. Cohen, L. O'Donnell, and I. Goodman. *Violence Prevention for Young Adolescents: A Survey of the State of the Art.* Available from the ERIC Clearinghouse (ED356442, 1991); 800-443-3742.

Peer Mediation Catches On, But Some Adults Don't

Edward Miller

One of the fastest-growing conflict resolution programs in schools is peer mediation, in which students are trained to mediate disputes between other students. There are now about 5,000 such programs in U.S. schools, up from just 100 five years ago, according to the National Association for Mediation in Education (NAME). In 1994, California Attorney General Daniel Lungren praised peer mediation as one of the most effective means to deter violence in public schools.

As with other school-based conflict resolution programs, however, there is no credible research evidence that peer mediation is able to prevent serious violence. Most evaluations are based on anecdotal evidence or comparisons of suspension rates in which the actual relationship among mediation, suspensions, and violence is unclear. "To date, there has not been a controlled study using randomly selected and randomly assigned students," says Dan Kmitta, NAME's research and evaluation coordinator. Peer mediation programs often receive glowing testimonials, of course, from the people who design and run them.

Some practitioners see a disturbing trend in the way these programs are being implemented in some schools. "Peer mediation," says Marvin Daniels, coordinator of the high school mediation program in Cambridge, Massachusetts, "has been misunderstood, misinterpreted, and transformed into something it was never meant to be. It is being used as a form of discipline, or as a prerequisite for suspension." Daniels sees mediation, used properly, as just one tool in a systematic campaign to begin changing the overall climate of violence in society.

Changing Adult Attitudes

It is the attitudes of adults, not those of students, that are most difficult to change, Daniels and other practitioners have found. "There are a lot of adults who don't want to give up power and authority to kids," notes Jo Ann Ezzo of the Cleveland Mediation Center. "Adults need to see kids as resources, not as problems," says Steven Brion-Meisels of the Risk and Prevention Program at the Harvard Graduate School of Education.

Some researchers like Joy Dryfoos, the author of *Adolescents at Risk* and *Full-Service Schools,* believe that peer mediation produces substantial benefit to the mediators themselves but little or no benefit to the disputants. Therefore, Dryfoos argues, for peer mediation to be effective in reducing violence it must be set up in a way that allows the high-risk students to be the mediators.

But this is precisely where adults are often reluctant to give up control of the process. "It's hard to get teachers to buy in to the idea that kids who are in trouble should be mediators," observes Sue Kohler, the mediation coordinator at Sycamore High School in Cincinnati. In some schools where high-risk students are trained as mediators, administrators nevertheless prevent them from hearing disputes by controlling the selection of mediators for individual cases.

"Adults must hold other adults accountable," argues Marvin Daniels. "You don't hear adults talk about accountability when it's adult to adult."

Though Daniels is encouraged by the growth of the mediation program in his own school—particularly by the fact that kids are starting to refer themselves to mediation when disputes arise—he sees the lack of adult accountability as contributing to the climate of violence in society. "The real sickness," he asserts, "is that we have adults who are making money off the marketability of violence. Who is holding those adults accountable—the adults who run the movie studios, the music business, the radio programs?"

"Kids and families are looking for alternatives to violence," says Brion-Meisels, "but society has not provided alternatives. Because of the images we get from the mass media, kids are good at envisioning violence and using the language of violence, but they are not good at envisioning images of peace."

Guidelines for Mediation

Practitioners like Ezzo, Kohler, and Daniels recommend the following guidelines for schools that want to set up effective peer mediation programs:

- Mediation should be just one aspect of a comprehensive school-wide philosophy of nonviolent conflict resolution that is reflected in the school's curriculum and policies.
- Parents and other community members should be included in the program.
- Mediators should be chosen from all racial, ethnic, and social groups in the school. In any one case, the makeup of the mediation team should match the disputants. For example, if the dispute is between a black student and a Latino student, there should be one black and one Latino mediator.
- High-risk students in particular—not just the "goody-goodies"—should be trained and used as mediators.
- Mediators should deal with real problems and disputes, not just trivial ones.
- Adult supervisors should not intervene during the mediation unless invited to do so by the student mediators.
- Teachers should be willing to adapt their schedules to accommodate mediation sessions.
- Mediation should not be used as a form of discipline, and students should not be coerced into using it. The process should be completely voluntary.

For Further Information

Child Development Project, Developmental Studies Center, 2000 Embarcadero, Oakland, CA 94606; 510-533-0213.

Children's Creative Response to Conflict Program, Box 271, Nyack, NY 10960; 914-358-4601.

Jo Ann Ezzo, Cleveland Mediation Center, 3000 Bridge Avenue, Cleveland, OH 44113; 216-771-7297.

National Association for Mediation in Education, 205 Hampshire House, Box 33635, Amherst, MA 01003-3635; 413-545-2462.

A. Steinberg. "Talking It Out: Students Mediate Disputes." *Harvard Education Letter* 5, no. 1 (January/February 1989).

We Need a National Strategy for Safe Schools

Gus Frias

The sixth of our National Education Goals calls for every school in America to be free of drugs and violence by the year 2000 and to offer a disciplined environment conducive to learning. The new Safe Schools Act allocates $20 million to this effort in the form of 20 one-year grants, intended to reinforce existing school safety programs.

As a 15-year veteran of efforts to prevent gang violence and create safe schools in southern California, I find the current legislation myopic and unrealistic. If we are truly serious about Goal Number 6 —if we are not just mouthing fine-sounding words—we must have a national strategy that creates a shared vision, includes every state (not just 20), and provides clear guidelines for safety initiatives at the individual school level. Such a strategy should include, at a minimum, three components:

1. Require the creation of comprehensive school safety plans at all public schools.

Every school administrator has a duty to protect the health and safety of his students and staff. An effective school safety plan includes the following elements:

- *Establish an interagency safe-school team at each site.* Start by identifying a group of highly committed individuals. The purpose of this team is to share responsibility and accountability for assessing risks and for planning, implementing, coordinating, and evaluating violence prevention efforts. Each team should have an administrator, a teacher, a parent, two students, the head custodian, a local businessperson, and a police officer.

- *Create a violence prevention vision.* Unity of vision is necessary for sacrifice and for action. This vision must be multidisciplinary in the interrelated areas of suppression, intervention, and prevention.
- *Establish goals and objectives.* The school safety plan must start with clear, realistic, and measurable goals to address the emotional, spiritual, and physical needs of students and their families. For example, older students can be trained to mentor younger ones on coping with pain and adversity at home and at school. The goal that every student should either be or have a mentor can be stated and the results tracked.
- *Create a detailed plan of action.* Delegate duties and responsibilities to each team member with specific timelines for completion.
- *Train teachers.* All educators need to know what is expected of them in preventing and responding to school crime and violence. Training should emphasize protective strategies and include crisis management and cultural awareness activities, where appropriate.
- *Educate parents.* All parents should be taught ways they can help prevent violence and recognize early indicators of drug abuse and gang activity. They need to know how the law applies to them and their children and what resources are available in the school and community to support them.
- *Develop student leadership.* Create a leadership class that meets daily for 25 of the school's most influential students. Half should be from the group considered to be at high risk. The purpose is to nurture a cadre of responsible students who will assist in violence prevention work.
- *Adopt a violence prevention curriculum.* Include the teaching of responsible citizenship, the strength of cultural diversity, choices and consequences, and conflict resolution skills. A good curriculum is incremental, age-appropriate, culturally sensitive, teacher-friendly, and consistent with other home and community initiatives. Most important, it should be integrated into the school's existing curriculum framework.
- *Prepare for crises.* Examine all existing plans for responding to a crisis. Analyze real-life cases. Identify a team of respond-

ers with clearly defined duties and roles. Conduct a crisis drill, evaluate the results, and modify the plans. This part of the plan should be directed by the team's law-enforcement representative.

- *Offer after-school activities for students.* These should include both recreation and tutoring. Provide mentors to help students with homework and to organize sports. Keep the school grounds open until 8 p.m.
- *Create school-business partnerships.* These can be sources of both after-school mentors and employment apprenticeship programs for students and their families.
- *Build a strong interagency team structure.* Review the team's expectations and limitations and discuss ways to adapt them. Create memorandums of understanding and seek court orders, if necessary, to facilitate the sharing of confidential information about crime and violence on or near school grounds.

2. Remove a school's immunity if administrators fail to create a school safety plan.

Many schools currently rely on the presence of just one police officer to address school safety. Therefore, if a violent incident occurs and that officer is not available, the school is unprepared. Other schools offer semi-annual one-hour violence prevention assemblies for teachers, students, and parents. These serve little purpose but to limit the school's legal liability in case of a violent incident. At some schools, administrators are still in a state of total denial and take no action at all.

School officials must be compelled to take their duty of care and responsibility seriously. If a child or teacher is killed on school grounds and no safety plan was in place, "I'm sorry" is simply not good enough. We must enforce a higher standard, including holding officials legally liable when they fail to adopt comprehensive school safety plans.

3. Create a national team-training academy.

Educators and community leaders alike need help in learning how to work together. Interagency personnel, in particular, face enormous barriers rooted in egoistic, territorial, and distrustful thinking. A national academy for training violence prevention teams could help us understand each other's strengths and weaknesses and learn to trust each other.

Exercising leadership in a violent environment is dangerous. We must learn the lessons of the past to avoid making deadly errors. The world does not need martyrs. It needs living heroes and heroines who can teach young people to reject violent, self-destructive behavior and to embrace life, education, family, and community. Making this happen will require brains, faith, and courage.

Part IV:
Dealing
With Abuse
And Harassment

The Physically or Sexually Abused Child: What Teachers Need To Know

Richard Fossey

One million children are victims of abuse or neglect each year in the United States—and those are just the confirmed cases. Experts agree that millions of other cases go unreported. One-fourth of the cases we know about involve serious physical abuse; another 15 percent, sexual abuse.

Abused children come from all kinds of families, but almost all have one thing in common: they go to school. For many of these children, caring teachers and counselors offer the best hope of relief and protection. Indeed, teachers in all 50 states have a legal obligation to report suspicions of child abuse to the police or child welfare authorities. Yet research shows that three out of four teachers may be unable to recognize the signs of abuse, even in obvious cases.

To encourage reporting, all states grant teachers immunity from lawsuits concerning any child-abuse report made in good faith, even when the report is mistaken and causes wrongly accused people considerable anguish. Still, many teachers wonder how sure they must be before they are required to report suspected abuse. Most authorities agree that educators should report if they have any "reasonable" suspicion. As one court explained, the reporting laws are intended to have a "low threshold for reporting" and only a minimum level of accuracy. Moreover, a knowing failure to report can lead to a fine, jail sentence, or both. In short, teachers should err on the side of reporting.

In spite of these laws and their immunity provisions, many teachers fail to act on their suspicions. Thomas McIntyre of Hunter College found that, although at least half of the nation's abused and ne-glected children are in school on any given day, only 10 percent of abuse and neglect reports originate in schools. Most of the teachers in his study said they had never had an abused or neglected child in their classrooms. Yet abuse is rampant. David Finkelhor of the Uni-versity of New Hampshire reviewed 19 studies published since 1983 and concluded that at least 20 percent of American women and between 5 percent and 10 percent of men were sexually abused in childhood by an adult.

The teachers McIntyre surveyed were shockingly ignorant of the signs of sexual abuse. Only 4 percent were "very aware" of such signs; 17 percent were able to recognize the signs if they were obvious; and 75 percent could not recognize signs of sexual abuse at any point. Moreover, Finkelhor and other researchers see evidence of a "back-lash" in current attitudes toward child sexual abuse—fed by sensa-tionalized news stories about miscarriages of justice in child welfare practices—that magnifies the effects of ignorance and indifference.

Educators should know the common indicators of abuse, but it is just as important that they understand the dynamics of abuse and the psychological effect it has on children. Those who do will not only be more likely to detect and report abuse, but will also be better able to develop teaching strategies to help abused children recover from their injuries. Our responsibility to an abused child does not end when the abuse is reported and stopped; we must nurture that child in ways that help him or her become a healthy, self-sufficient, and confident adult.

Isolation Is Common

Physical abuse seems most common in families of low socioeco-nomic status, but most researchers have concluded that child sexual abuse is unrelated to social class or family income. Finkelhor found no link between sexual abuse and parental education, income, or father's occupation.

But an abundance of studies have shown that child abuse victims are often socially isolated, regardless of their social class or economic status. Children who are abused by a parent are frequently prohib-ited from having close relationships outside the family. Such children may also isolate themselves because of the shame associated with victimization by a family member.

Children who are abused by nonfamily members are often isolated from their parents. Finkelhor hypothesized that children with poor parental relationships may be emotionally deprived and needy, and thus more vulnerable to an abuser's offers of friendship and appreciation. Moreover, children with poor parental relationships may be afraid to tell their parents about the abuse because they think they will not be believed or supported. Finkelhor concluded that a poor relationship with one's parents was one of the strongest correlates of sexual abuse among girls.

Abused children may also be isolated from friends. A recent study conducted by Suzanne Salzinger and colleagues at the New York State Psychiatric Institute found that children who are physically abused at home are often unpopular with classmates. Parents and teachers were more likely to describe them as disturbed. "Abused children [in the Salzinger study] did not seem to know who their friends were," reported the *Harvard Mental Health Letter.* "The children they named as friends often rejected them and there were usually other classmates who liked them better. Other children rarely made this kind of social misjudgment."

It seems likely that sexual abusers who are not related to their victims choose isolated children as their targets to reduce the risk of discovery. The victims often come from dysfunctional families. Robin Cona, a legal adviser for the Illinois Board of Education, observes that sexually abusive teachers choose their victims carefully. "They zero in on the more vulnerable kids—the unhappy ones, the ones with no one to tell," she says.

Child abusers themselves confirm that they often look for particular characteristics in their potential victims. Sex offenders at the Maine State Prison, who created a handbook on child abuse prevention, described their victims in these words: "Someone who had been a victim before; quiet, withdrawn, compliant. . . . Easier to manipulate, less likely to put up a fight, goes along with things. . . . The look in their eyes. It's a look of trust. They like you. If they are going to show resistance, they'll look away."

This portrait of the victim as lonely, vulnerable, and isolated from family and friends may explain why sexual abuse often goes undetected for long periods. Victims may have no one to turn to for help and no one who is close enough emotionally to recognize their distress.

Abused children often exhibit academic or behavioral problems in school. Physically abused children have trouble solving problems with peers, and often lack close friends. A 1993 study by John Eckenrode and colleagues at Cornell University concluded that abused and neglected children were more likely than others to be poor learners, have discipline problems, and be retained in grade. Physically abused children, in particular, had high rates of discipline referrals and suspensions. On the other hand, the same study found that sexually abused children did not exhibit unusual academic or discipline problems, unless the children were neglected as well as sexually abused. One writer has noted that sexually abused adolescents may actually improve their school performance as a way of concealing the abuse.

Children with disabilities are at higher risk than others, suggesting that special education teachers be especially watchful for signs of abuse. Darcy Miller of Washington State University found that adolescents with behavioral disorders reported high incidences of both sexual and physical abuse.

The Legacy of Trauma

Abused children are victims of trauma. Judith Herman and colleagues at Harvard Medical School report that, although the impact depends on the child's developmental stage and the severity of the trauma, the effects of abuse are fairly predictable. Repeated physical and sexual abuse causes long-term psychological injury, which may in turn increase the victim's vulnerability to further abuse.

Chronic abuse impairs the child's intellectual and social development, preventing "the ordinary integration of knowledge, memory, emotional states, and bodily experience," says Herman. Other researchers have noted a similarity between the symptoms of trauma victims and attention deficit disorder, suggesting that for some children ADD may be linked to trauma. There is also evidence that abuse is a cause of childhood hyperactivity.

Bessel van der Kolk of Harvard Medical School believes that severe trauma creates physiological changes in the central nervous system that may manifest themselves at school as learning disorders. Abused children, researchers report, have impaired verbal ability; they speak fewer sentences, use fewer words, and do not enjoy inventing stories as much as other children. They have a harder time solving problems and give up easily.

There is good evidence that abused children sometimes develop a destructive attachment to their abusers, particularly if the abuser is a caregiver such as a parent or teacher. Sometimes this attachment prevents the victim from breaking free of the abuser and seeking help. "Even more than adults," says Judith Herman, "children who develop in a climate of domination develop pathological attachments to those who abuse and neglect them, attachments that they will strive to maintain even at the sacrifice of their own welfare, their own reality, or their lives."

Often this pathological attachment will cause an abused child to protect the abuser, sometimes by helping the abuser avoid detection. Arthur Green of Columbia University found that a child's tendency to shield an abusive parent may not be motivated solely by a desire to avoid harsher treatment. Rather, the child may be engaging in pervasive denial.

"This suppression of the perception of parental assault was occasionally motivated by threats of additional punishment," says Green, "but it also was associated with the children's desperate need to protect themselves from the terrifying awareness of the parents' destructive impulses toward them, the acknowledgment of which reality would lead to fears of annihilation, or intense retaliatory rage, which would endanger the child's psychological survival."

Finally, trauma victims have a tendency to re-expose themselves to situations that are reminiscent of the original trauma. Van der Kolk calls this phenomenon "addiction to trauma," and others have referred to it as "learned helplessness." Richard Kluft of Temple University studied incest victims who were later sexually exploited by therapists; he called the phenomenon "the sitting duck syndrome."

Indicators of Abuse

The signs of abuse are not always easy to see. Child abuse—particularly sexual abuse—usually takes place in secret, away from school. Nevertheless, there are certain indicators that teachers should know.

Unexplained bruises, welts, bite marks, burns, or fractures—especially if they appear regularly after school absences—may be indicators of physical abuse. Children who engage in self-destructive behavior, are chronic runaways, have unattended medical needs, or show a reluctance to go home at the end of the school day may also be victims of physical abuse.

Physically abused children often are wary of adult contact, are unusually apprehensive when other children are upset, give improbable explanations for or refuse to talk about injuries, and pretend that their injuries don't hurt.

Torn, stained, or bloody underclothing; venereal diseases; pain in the genital area; or difficulty walking or sitting may be indicators of sexual abuse. Children who attempt suicide, are threatened by physical contact, mimic sex acts, or behave promiscuously may also be showing the signs of victimization.

Sexually abused children often are unwilling to change clothes for or participate in gym, have poor relationships with peers, have a distorted body image (their artwork may depict missing or mutilated body parts), become aggressive or violent when provoked, or seem withdrawn, infantile, or depressed.

Though all educators are required to report suspected abuse, state laws vary somewhat in their definitions of abuse and neglect. School administrators have a legal and ethical duty to inform their staffs about applicable local laws and to mobilize teachers to become active protectors of children at risk.

For Further Information

J. Eckenrode, M. Laird, and J. Doris. "School Performance and Disciplinary Problems Among Abused and Neglected Children." *Developmental Psychology* 29, no. 1 (January 1993): 53-62.

A. Green. "Children Traumatized by Physical Abuse." In S. Eth and R. Pynoos (eds.), *Post-Traumatic Stress Disorder in Children.* Washington, DC: American Psychiatric Press, 1985.

J. Herman. *Trauma and Recovery.* New York: Basic Books, 1992.

T. McIntyre. "The Teacher's Role in Cases of Suspected Child Abuse." *Education and Urban Society* 22, no. 3 (May 1990): 300-306.

S. Salzinger et al. "The Effects of Physical Abuse on Children's Social Relationships." *Child Development* 64, no. 1 (February 1993): 169-187.

G. Sorenson. "Sexual Abuse in Schools: Reported Cases from 1987-1990." *Educational Administration Quarterly* 27, no. 4 (November 1991): 460-480.

Courts Hold Coworkers Liable for Knowledge Of Sexual Abuse

Richard Fossey

E ducators are often reluctant to confront the fact that some children are abused at school by teachers or other adults. Several recent court decisions underscore the urgent need for teachers and administrators to stop looking the other way.

We do not know the extent of child abuse in schools, but most experts agree that coerced sex between school personnel and students is not rare. Students are reluctant to report such crimes, and officials who discover them often handle matters quietly to avoid publicity. A 1993 survey reported that 21 percent of females and 8 percent of males in grades 8 through 11 had been sexually harassed by a school employee. Other researchers have found that 1 percent to 3 percent of all children are molested by an adult at school.

The catastrophic effects of such abuse on students are, of course, the main reason to stop it. Another is legal liability. Courts have become more willing in recent years to hold coworkers responsible for an abusive employee's action if it is shown that they knew about the abuse and did nothing.

For many years state courts have been reluctant to take this step. Several state courts have ruled that school employees act outside the scope of their employment when they commit a sexual assault, and thus school districts may not be held accountable. Moreover, in many jurisdictions, school boards and employees are immune from negligence suits.

Abused children and their families have begun suing school boards and employees in the federal courts, with some success. A federal appellate court ruled, in *Stoneking v. Bradford Area School*

District (1989), that a public school principal could be held liable for damages in a case where a former high school student charged that she had been assaulted by the school band director for three years and that the principal was aware of the accusations but failed to investigate them.

In *Jane Doe v. Taylor (Texas) Independent School District* (1994), the Fifth Circuit Court of Appeals issued a similar ruling. In that case, a student claimed that the principal failed to protect her from a teacher's sexual advances in spite of reports to the principal about the teacher's misconduct from the school librarian, a counselor, two community members, and at least one student.

A school employee who sexually assaults a student violates Title IX of the Education Amendments of 1972, the federal law that prohibits sex discrimination in schools that receive federal funds. The U.S. Supreme Court ruled in 1992, in a case involving accusations of sexual harassment and abuse by a teacher, that school districts could be sued under Title IX for the full range of compensatory and punitive damages.

Until recently, most questions of liability involved supervisors and school boards. But a federal court in Texas ruled in *Doe v. Rains Independent School District* (1994) that a molester's teaching colleagues can also be held liable if they knew that a student was being sexually abused and failed to report it in accordance with state law.

How Abuse Happens

These and other cases tell us much about how sexual abuse happens in schools. It usually involves multiple incidents and multiple victims. A survey by Gail Sorenson of the University of North Carolina found 37 cases over a four-year period; 20 involved multiple victims, and 30 involved multiple acts of abuse against the same student. Sorenson's findings suggest that sexual abuse often goes on for a long time—months or even years—without detection.

Child abuse in schools is often a crime of opportunity. Certain job categories figure prominently in cases of sexual abuse and harassment: male coaches, band directors, and extracurricular advisers. These adults tend to be held in high regard by students and have more opportunities for one-to-one contact with them—often in private settings—than other teachers. Coaches and band directors usually have access to isolated facilities such as training and dressing rooms, empty gyms, and band practice rooms. Court records show that sexual assaults often take place in these settings.

Studies show that children with physical and mental disabilities and behavioral disorders may be particularly vulnerable to sexual abuse. Several cases involve accusations that the abuse took place while such students were being transported to or from school.

Finally, court records suggest that sexual abuse by school employees is more likely to happen where there is a climate of indifference toward such acts—where officials failed to respond to reports of abuse. School boards manifest this same indifference when they enter into confidential agreements with teachers accused of sexual abuse, allowing them to go to other districts where they molest still more children.

These patterns of behavior suggest certain basic precautions. In general, a school employee should not be left alone with a single child in an isolated setting for long periods. Extra care should be taken in supervising special education students at school and in transit. Given the tendency of abusers to have multiple victims, authorities should thoroughly investigate an employee's activities after a single incident of abuse is discovered. Schools should also regularly inform employees of their legal responsibility to report child abuse.

Perhaps most important, school leaders should remind employees of their obligation to respect and protect the children in their care. We may never be able to eradicate sexual abuse in schools, but we can and must nurture school cultures that are intolerant of adults who exploit children.

Sexual Harassment at An Early Age: New Cases Are Changing the Rules For Schools

Susan Eaton

Second-grader Cheltzie Hentz of Eden Prairie, Minnesota, couldn't understand why the boys on the school bus screamed the word "bitch" at her and the other little girls. Each day, the boys taunted seven-year-old Cheltzie and her friends for being girls—for having "stinky vaginas" instead of penises. The bus driver, Cheltzie says, seemed to think it was all a joke.

But Cheltzie and her mother, Sue Mutziger, weren't laughing. They sent repeated explicit letters about the incidents to school officials and eventually filed complaints with the state Department of Human Rights and with the U.S. Education Department's Office for Civil Rights. School officials did remove some of the offending boys from the bus, but, Mutziger says, that failed to stop the harassment.

"The day it hit me," Mutziger recalls, "was when Cheltzie said, 'Mom, I guess that's just the way boys are supposed to talk to girls, isn't it?' Then I realized how conditioned she was to this—how it seemed normal to her. And I got angry."

The U.S. Department of Education ruled in April 1993 that the Eden Prairie Schools had violated federal law in "failing to take timely and effective responsive action to address . . . multiple or severe acts of sexual harassment" perpetrated against eight girls, including Cheltzie Hentz. It was the first federal finding of student-to-student sexual harassment at the elementary school level. The ruling puts school administrators at every grade level on notice: the Department of Education is taking sexual harassment complaints very seriously.

The Eden Prairie district agreed to develop new written guide-lines to assist staff in recognizing and stopping sexual harassment, to keep better records of complaints and corrective actions, including informal ones, and to monitor and assess the effectiveness of its efforts. The district will continue to be monitored by the Office for Civil Rights.

Across the country, girls like Cheltzie are talking more openly about the sexual harassment they experience on the buses, in the classrooms and hallways, and on the playing fields and playgrounds of daily school life. As educators begin to realize that sexual harass-ment does happen in school, they confront not only complex legal issues but fundamental questions about how to foster equality and respect in a society that often dismisses catcalls, pinching, bra-snap-ping, and even breast-twisting as "boys being boys."

Students Harassing Students

Nan Stein of the Center for Research on Women at Wellesley College refers to sexual harassment as "a well-known social secret," something that happens all the time in schools but is ignored or brushed off because girls may not know the name for it, or may be afraid of causing trouble over "nothing." Teachers may accept it as natural, ritualistic behavior.

Sexual harassment should not be confused with flirting, which makes people feel good. Rather, it is unwelcome attention that the victim feels she cannot stop. Harassment includes blatant offenses, such as a teacher demanding sex in return for a good grade. But research and legal cases are increasingly exposing the more common kinds of harassment that occur between students.

A 1993 nationwide survey of 1,632 randomly selected public school students in grades 8 through 11, commissioned by the Ameri-can Association of University Women, found that sexual harassment in school is epidemic, and that boys as well as girls are victims. The survey showed, however, that the effects of harassment on girls are much more severe.

Eighty-five percent of the girls and 76 percent of the boys sur-veyed in this study reported being sexually harassed in school. One-fourth of the students said they were harassed "often." The most common forms of harassment reported were sexual comments, jokes, and gestures (66 percent); being touched, grabbed, or pinched in a sexual way (53 percent); and being intentionally brushed up against in a sexual way (46 percent). Many students also reported being "flashed" or "mooned," being the targets of sexual rumors, and having their clothing pulled at or off.

Peer harassment was found to be more than four times as common as adult harassment. Three out of five students admitted having sexually harassed others. Only 7 percent of the victims said they had told a teacher about the harassment.

One-third of the students said they had first experienced sexual harassment in grade 6 or earlier. Sixty percent had experienced harassment by grade 8.

Victims vary in their emotional responses to sexual harassment, but there are some common reactions. According to Kathy Hotelling of Northern Illinois University, self-esteem and confidence in both academic work and personal relationships are likely to plummet, and other responses may include anger, hurt, depression, decreased concentration, listlessness, and a feeling of being trapped. Victims tend to focus on avoiding the harasser, rather than on schoolwork and normal relationships with peers and adults.

The most common academic effects of harassment reported by students in the 1993 AAUW survey were "not wanting to come to school," "not wanting to talk as much in class," and "finding it hard to pay attention in school." In each case, girls reported these effects two to three times more often than boys. There was a similar divergence in the reporting of emotional impact; twice as many girls as boys reported feeling embarrassed, self-conscious, and less sure of themselves because of sexual harassment in school. For boys, the most disturbing form of harassment was being called gay.

Professor Stephanie Riger of the University of Illinois at Chicago reports that victims often blame themselves for the incidents and feel powerless and ashamed. Sexual harassment, says Hotelling, "reduces the quality of education, diminishes academic achievement, and ultimately may lower earning power."

A Sexually Hostile Environment

Sexual harassment is a violation of Title IX of the Education Amendments of 1972, Title VII of the Civil Rights Act, and the Equal Protection Clause of the Fourteenth Amendment. Under Title IX, any school district that receives federal education funds is held directly responsible for the discriminatory acts of its employees. This clearly covers sexual harassment by a teacher or other adult, directed at either a student or a co-worker.

Educators really began to take notice after the U.S. Supreme Court ruled in February 1992, in *Franklin v. Gwinnett County Public Schools,* that a school can be forced to pay damages to the victim of sexual harassment. Previously, Title IX was thought to provide only "equitable" relief—an order to stop the harassment, for example, or back pay to an employee who left her job because of harassment. *Gwinnett* raised the possibility of huge damage suits against school districts and administrators. Significantly, the Supreme Court's decision in the case was unanimous.

But *Gwinnett* was a case of harassment of a student by an employee, not by other students. Now, with the Eden Prairie case, the Office for Civil Rights (OCR) maintains that a district also violates Title IX "when it knew or should have known that a sexually hostile environment exists due to student-to-student harassment and fails to take timely and effective corrective action." Whether Title IX could lead to damage claims against schools in such cases awaits further clarification by the courts.

Another important question is the definition of a "sexually hostile environment." The OCR defines it as one characterized "by acts of a sexual nature that are sufficiently severe or pervasive to impair the educational benefits" offered by the school. "The existence of a sexually hostile environment," the OCR continues, "is determined from the viewpoint of a reasonable person in the victim's situation." The OCR specifically includes school buses among the settings in which illegal sexual harassment can occur.

Some court decisions, however, seem to be in conflict with the OCR interpretation. The U.S. Court of Appeals for the Second Circuit ruled, in a case involving Yale University, that under Title IX the harassment had to be so severe as to deny completely the educational benefits to the student—by forcing her, for example, to drop out of school.

Policy and Practice

An essential part of addressing the problem, experts agree, is for every school to have a clear written policy on sexual harassment. A good policy would define different kinds of harassment, with examples, and would explicitly prohibit such harassment between staff members, between staff and students, and among students them-selves. It should also provide victims with a range of options for stopping the harassing behavior.

Minuteman Regional Vocational Technical High School in Lex-ington, Massachusetts has a long-standing policy that is often cited as a model (see "Guidelines for Recognizing and Dealing with Sexual Harassment," page 107). Minuteman administrators advise schools to identify several adults as "complaint managers." With several to choose from, a student can report harassment to the adult with whom she feels most comfortable.

Psychologists like Stephanie Riger point out that women are often discouraged from reporting incidents of harassment if the only avenues for redress are legal action or filing a formal grievance. Some schools have adopted informal resolution processes for students who feel they are being harassed by a peer. Such resolutions might include a letter to the accused harasser. The complaint manager may deliver the letter, or accompany the victim when she delivers it.

Avoiding Liability

Though having a written policy on harassment is essential, that alone cannot protect a school district from legal liability. School staff must understand what the policy means and how to apply it. The Eden Prairie district had in fact adopted a policy prohibiting sexual harassment between students, but the Office for Civil Rights found that the district's response to complaints was flawed by its failure to identify the incidents as sexual harassment and then to follow its own procedures. As a result, school officials treated the incidents as in-stances of using bad language rather than as sexual harassment.

Eden Prairie district personnel told investigators that they con-sidered the sexual harassment policy to apply only to overt displays of sexual aggression or unwelcome solicitation. Particularly with young children, they were inclined to treat offensive sex talk as "inappropriate behavior or language" rather than as violations of the harassment policy.

But the Office for Civil Rights ruled that, looking at the case from the standpoint of the victims, sexual harassment had clearly oc-curred, regardless of the age of the harassers. "The fact that neither the boys nor the girls were sufficiently mature to realize all of the meanings and nuances of the language that was used does not obvi-ate a finding that sexual harassment occurred," wrote Kenneth

Mines, regional director of the agency, in his finding. "In this case, there is no question that even the youngest girls understood that the language and conduct being used were expressions of hostility toward them on the basis of their sex."

It is thus important for teachers and administrators to recognize that harassment occurs at all levels of a school system and should be named and addressed as such. Moreover, policies and procedures alone are not enough. Principals and other school leaders should state publicly that sexual harassment is a serious issue and will not be tolerated in their schools. They should also be able to explain clearly why such behavior is unacceptable. But strong statements have to be backed up by curricular changes, schoolwide discussions, staff training, and emotional support for victims.

"Administration has a lot of power in setting a tone," says Susan Strauss, author of *Sexual Harassment and Teens: A Program for Positive Change.* "But then they have to turn around and see what else really needs to be done to make the culture change." In schools where leaders have not addressed the issue, Strauss suggests, the recent legal rulings provide a natural starting point for teachers and lower-level administrators to begin raising awareness of sexual harassment.

"You certainly don't have to be an administrator to start this," says Strauss. "There is a legal obligation for every adult in the school."

Making Lasting Change

A big challenge facing educators is that many boys and young men do not understand why their behavior is defined as harassment. They may consider catcalls and leers harmless, or even complimentary. For that reason, a policy that is merely punitive and not aimed at changing behavior won't work. Ideally, classroom activities should encourage students to examine sexist behavior and to figure out for themselves why it is offensive.

"If there is no education in advance," says Stein, "if students don't know when their own behavior is harassing, punishing them doesn't make sense."

At Minuteman, the harassment policy is linked to workshops for staff and students. Administrators find that "preventive training" is most effective when it acknowledges that sexual harassment is a cultural problem rather than simply the failure of the school or the individual harasser.

Guidelines for Recognizing and Dealing with Sexual Harassment

Following are excerpts from Minuteman Regional Vocational Technical High School's sexual harassment policy. The full text of Minuteman's policy is included in *Who's Hurt and Who's Liable* (see "For Further Information," page 109).

Definition: Sexual harassment is unwanted sexual attention from peers, subordinates, supervisors, customers, clients, or anyone the victim may interact with in order to fill job or school duties. . . . The range of behaviors includes: verbal comments, subtle pressure for sexual activity, leering, pinching, patting, and other forms of unwanted touching. . . .

Dimension of the problem: Sexual harassment is a problem in every school as well as in every workplace. Students experience it from other students and occasionally from faculty members.

Effects on the victim: The victim may be in the office or school less in order to avoid the harassment (more sick days taken). The victim's enjoyment of and pride in work is often undermined or destroyed because the victim is forced to spend time and energy fending off humiliating sexual advances. There can also be physical and psychological effects similar to those experienced by rape victims. Professional counseling may be necessary.

Grievance procedures: When the complaint has come from a female student or faculty member, a female counselor or a female member of the Title IX Committee should be present at all discussions and meetings involving the case. . . . It is particularly important . . . to have a supportive representative or counselor present during the investigation to make it easier for the student to discuss such a delicate issue. . . .

Retaliation: Retaliation in any form against any person who has filed a complaint relating to sexual harassment is forbidden. . . . It could be considered grounds for removal from the educational setting for a student.

Confidentiality: It is expected that those involved with sexual harassment investigations will protect the confidentiality of all information relating to the case.

While schools have just begun grappling with this issue, there are some emerging examples of how to reduce sexual harassment in schools. The Massachusetts Department of Education has published a curriculum guide, "Who's Hurt and Who's Liable," with materials that can be incorporated into lessons on sex stereotyping, workers' rights, and violence prevention. In one section, students take on the role of "Susan," an auto shop student who is being harassed. The situation is based on an actual case.

Students may find it easiest to talk about sexual harassment at first by recounting their own experiences or simply by offering their own opinions on what constitutes harassment and then arguing about them. Experts say that students find the issue more relevant if harassment is first discussed in the context of their own school. Later the discussion can move to harassment in the workplace and in society in general.

Author Susan Strauss runs school workshops in which students list the differences between harassment and flirting. Strauss describes various scenarios and then asks students to decide whether what has taken place is flirting or harassment. She also uses a true-false questionnaire to assess students' knowledge and attitudes. One statement is: "Most girls like getting sexual attention at work and at school."

"School is a microcosm of society," says Strauss. "Obviously, nothing we do is going to completely eliminate sexual harassment. But a lot of schools are taking notice."

As the Eden Prairie case shows, taking notice is only the first step. Indeed, a 1992 survey by the Minnesota attorney general's office found that 88 percent of the 340 schools canvassed had posted sexual harassment policies, but only 38 percent said that the policies were "well understood." Understanding will come much more slowly.

For Further Information

Hostile Hallways: The AAUW Survey on Sexual Harassment in America's Schools. American Association of University Women, P.O. Box 251, Annapolis Junction, MD 20701-0251; 800-225-9998. 1993, $11.95.

It's Not Fun—It's Illegal: The Identification and Prevention of Sexual Harassment to Teenagers. Minnesota Department of Education, 522 Capitol Square Building, 550 Cedar St., St. Paul, MN 55101, 1988; 612-297-2792. $10.

J. Lewis, S. Hastings, and A. Morgan. *Sexual Harassment in Education.* Topeka: National Organization on Legal Problems of Education, 1992; 913-273-3550.

No Laughing Matter: High School Students and Sexual Harassment. 25-minute videotape. Massachusetts Department of Education, 350 Main St., Malden, MA 02148, 1982. $25.

N. Stein. "It Happens Here, Too: Sexual Harassment and Child Sexual Abuse in Elementary and Secondary Schools," in *Gender and Education,* S. K. Biklen and D. Pollard, eds. Chicago: National Society for the Study of Education, 1993 yearbook.

S. Strauss and P. Espeland. *Sexual Harassment and Teens: A Program for Positive Change.* Free Spirit Publishing, 400 First Avenue North, Suite 616, Minneapolis, MN 55401, 1992; 1-800-735-7323.

Tune In to Your Rights. A Guide for Teenagers About Turning Off Sexual Harassment. Programs for Educational Opportunity, 1005 School of Education Building, University of Michigan, Ann Arbor, MI 48109, 1985; 313-763-9910. Spanish edition available. $3.

Who's Hurt and Who's Liable: Sexual Harassment in Massachusetts Schools. A Curriculum Guide for School Personnel. Massachusetts Department of Education, 350 Main St., Malden, MA 02148, 1986. Free.

Sexual Harassment: Lisa's Complaint

Edward Miller

The following case is based on actual incidents. It is presented here as a conversation starter—designed to provoke discussion by school faculties and students. Names and other identifying details have been changed to protect the privacy of those involved.

Lisa Jackson, 14, kept her eyes glued to the poem that Mr. Wickman had just asked the ninth-grade English class to read, but she couldn't shut out the kissing and sucking sounds coming from behind her. She remembered her friend Joanne's advice: "The creeps just want to see you react. Don't give them the satisfaction."

The sounds changed to heavy breathing and low moaning. Lisa's face flushed. Finally she turned her head and whispered, "Stop it, Bobby."

Bobby Marshall, who sat directly behind Lisa, chuckled and looked at his friend Richard in the next row. He and Richard were teammates on the freshman football squad.

Bobby leaned forward and made a lewd comment about Lisa's breasts. He spoke just loudly enough for Richard to hear. The boys giggled and sputtered.

Lisa looked up at Mr. Wickman with a pleading expression just as he asked the class, "Who's finished reading the poem?" Peering out from behind his desk at the front of the room, he saw Lisa's upturned face and said, "Lisa? Good. Will you tell us what you think the poet means here by the word *sleep*?"

Lisa looked down again quickly, ashamed and confused, and said nothing. Mr. Wickman made a mark in his daily grade book. Behind Lisa, Bobby said, "I'll see you in my wet dreams, baby."

* * * * *

Ann Danton, the guidance counselor, said to Assistant Principal Caroline Morgan, "I think you ought to talk to Lisa Jackson. After the assembly on the new sexual harassment policy, she gave me the impression that she might be a victim. I've been worried about her anyway. She's failing English and math. She's always struggled with language arts, but I feel she could be doing better. Something's troubling her."

Caroline retrieved Lisa's file. Her grades were mostly C's and D's, but there was no disciplinary record. Her teachers described her as "immature" and "lacking social skills."

Soon Lisa was sitting nervously in the young assistant principal's office. Caroline closed the door. "Lisa, you were at the assembly when I explained the definition of sexual harassment, weren't you?" Lisa nodded. "Is somebody doing that to you?"

Lisa looked as if she were about to cry. "Yes," she said at last, "but I shouldn't have said anything to Ms. Danton. I don't want to get anyone in trouble."

Caroline moved her chair closer and put her arm around the girl. She again explained the school's policy on harassment, emphasizing that the first step in making a complaint did not involve punishment. "You're not getting anybody in trouble," she said. "You're the one who's got the trouble, and it's important to do something about it."

After much prodding and encouragement, Lisa poured out the whole story. Bobby, Richard, and three other boys had been making sexual comments for several weeks. Bobby had also pushed Lisa up against her locker and squeezed her breast and buttocks. The latest thing was the noises in class.

Caroline was a little surprised when she heard the boys' names. They were not what she would call "troubled" kids; they were "regular" guys, well liked by students and staff.

Caroline and Lisa pulled their chairs up to the computer and called up the sexual harassment memo format that the principal's harassment task force had developed. Though Lisa struggled to find the right words, with Caroline's help she wrote a memo to Bobby and the other boys, following the format called for in the harassment policy. She described in specific, graphic detail what they had said and done, how it had made her feel, and what she wanted them to do about it.

"When you said 'I'll see you in my wet dreams' in English class on Monday," she wrote, "I felt embarrassed and dirty. When you made sucking sounds and talked about my 'tits' I felt angry and ashamed. And when you pushed me and touched me in the hallway last week I was afraid. I don't want you to say those things anymore and I don't want you to do those things anymore."

*   *   *   *   *

Lisa sat pensively reading the finished memo over and over. She knew that the next step was for Caroline, as assistant principal, to deliver the memo in person to each of the boys and to warn them officially. Though there would be no punishment or disciplinary hearing at this stage, if Caroline received any further complaints of sexual harassment about them she would take formal action.

But Caroline needed Lisa's permission to deliver the memo.

"No, I can't do it," Lisa finally said. "This paper will just make things worse. I don't know what they might do to me. Please, Ms. Morgan, don't say anything to them."

Nothing Caroline could say would change Lisa's mind. And the school policy strictly prohibited delivering Lisa's memo without her written permission.

*   *   *   *   *

Some questions raised by this case:
1. What, if anything, should Caroline Morgan do now?
2. How realistic are Lisa's fears of retaliation?
3. What are the school's legal and ethical responsibilities toward the students involved in the case?
4. Are there problems with this school's policy on sexual harassment?

Gay Students Find Little Support In Most Schools

Susan Eaton

On the first day of the school year, a 16-year-old student at a public high school outside Washington, DC, finds the word "faggot" etched on his locker. "I told some people just to test it out, I guess," the student says. "I thought I could trust them. I thought the keeping it inside. . . . I thought nothing could be worse."

In Vermont, a lesbian teenager, not a victim of violence or harassment, drops out of school anyway, feeling "separate from everyone . . . alone. It was that I couldn't be me," she explains.

Psychological research and published life stories of gay and lesbian people confirm that school can be an unwelcoming, even dangerous place for young homosexuals, who, like all adolescents, are struggling to be accepted and to accept themselves. Even students who may not be homosexual but are confused about sexual identity—a common experience in adolescence—may withdraw or become depressed and anxious in an environment that is disapproving of, perhaps even hostile to, the question "Could I be gay?"

Some gay and lesbian students are verbally and physically abused by classmates. Teachers and administrators do not usually promote the abuse, but they may nevertheless condone it. School rules and regulations—not to mention enlightened attitudes—may put an end to hateful notes, name-calling, and defaced lockers. But some educators see a need to do more.

Few Happy Memories

The percentage of gays and lesbians in the teenage and adult population is a matter of dispute. Estimates range from one percent to the 10 percent figure first proposed by Alfred Kinsey after a famous study. This means that between 315,000 and 3.15 million teens in the U.S. are gay.

Whatever estimate one chooses to accept, the anguish suffered by these students is underscored by a U.S. Department of Health and Human Services (HHS) study revealing that gay and lesbian youth account for about one-third of all teen suicides and are two to three times more likely than their straight peers to attempt suicide.

None of the 44 adult gay men and lesbians interviewed in 1991, in a small but significant survey conducted through the University of Southern Maine, said they had had good experiences in high school. Only a few reported any positive mention of homosexuality by adults in high school. On the contrary, locker defacement, notes, taunting, and even beatings are common. A study by the National Gay and Lesbian Task Force found that 45 percent of gay men and 20 percent of lesbians experienced verbal or physical assault in high school. About 28 percent eventually drop out of school, according to the HHS study.

Of course, many problems a gay teenager faces are identical to those of any adolescent. Psychological studies of gay and lesbian students describe low self-esteem and feelings of inadequacy, problems that are common to most teens. Like all adolescents, gay and lesbian teenagers seek intimate relationships and confiding friendships in which they can be known and valued for their true selves.

But the problems and desires of adolescence are exaggerated for young homosexuals and teens who are unsure about their sexual orientation. These students learn quickly that their feelings run counter to what is accepted and valued at home, in school, in church, and in society. Many gay men and lesbians report having sensed something "different" about themselves as early as age five. According to a study by Emory Hetrick and A. Damien Martin published in the *Journal of Homosexuality,* about 80 percent of lesbian, gay, and bisexual youths report "severe" problems of isolation. These include having no one to talk to, feeling distanced from family and peers, and lacking access to good information about sexual orientation.

Teenage friendships and intense peer group discussions often center on heterosexual dating. This often leaves gay or lesbian teens without a place to explore, test, or talk about their feelings of sexual attraction to or affection for their own sex. Homosexual youngsters are, therefore, left out of a shared experience that for heterosexual teens creates bonds, feelings of maturity, and an acknowledgment that they are "okay."

If gay or lesbian adolescents discuss their feelings with family members, they may be doubly rejected, or sent to a therapist to "correct" what parents see as a problem. A 1987 study by Gary Remafedi found that about half of gay and lesbian youths say they were rejected by their parents. The HHS study revealed that 26 percent of gay and lesbian youth are forced to leave home because of family conflict over sexual identity. Feeling alone and different, many gay and lesbian teens begin to hate themselves and try to drown out the feelings with drugs, alcohol, and even suicide.

Schools Can Hurt—and Help

Schools contribute to these overwhelming feelings of isolation in several ways, say youth workers and social psychologists. Some gay rights activists call schools "heterosexist," meaning that they operate on the assumption that everyone is heterosexual.

Gilbert Herdt of the University of Chicago found that this "presumption of heterosexuality" has a profound effect on an adolescent's emerging identity. It can cause a student to hide his or her sexual orientation and to feign heterosexuality, says Herdt, and may lead to severe identity confusion, resentment, and distrust.

School officials sometimes tolerate name-calling that becomes pervasive in hallways and on playing fields. Students may use labels like "queer," "faggot," or "lezzie" as all-purpose putdowns, not necessarily directed at someone who is gay or lesbian. These epithets, say gay and lesbian students and their advocates, are tolerated in schools in a way profanity or racial slurs are not.

There are various ways in which schools can become less hostile environments for these students. For one thing, youth workers and others recommend that school officials adopt—and enforce—clear policies explicitly forbidding such insulting or threatening words and actions against homosexuals. Subtler measures can also be helpful. Surveys show that something as simple as seeing a book on gay teens or a positive poster in a counselor's office can make students feel more welcome.

School people need to become more aware of what contributes to a "heterosexist" environment. "Sometimes it's the language that's being used—nothing derogatory, but just not inclusive," says Jerri Lynn Fields, director of youth services for Horizons, a social service agency for gay and lesbian people in Chicago. "Sometimes it's just a matter of using the word 'partner' instead of 'husband' or 'wife.' "

And school leaders, when talking about valuing diversity, should make it clear that gay and lesbian students and teachers are part of the community. Virginia Uribe, the founder of a school-based support group for gay and lesbian high school students in Los Angeles called Project 10, points out that "just saying those words—gay and lesbian—is terribly important."

Curriculum Options

Many advocates believe that even if a school does forbid name-calling and other harassment, failing to mention "those words—gay and lesbian" makes homosexual students feel invisible. According to Arthur Lipkin, a research associate at Harvard University, positive and accurate discussions of gay life and literature are generally lacking in schools across the country. Furthermore, he says, teachers who want to change things find few guides and little reliable information.

To remedy this situation, Lipkin has written several units on gay and lesbian history and life to be incorporated into classes in standard subjects. For example, one social studies unit, designed to take eight to ten days, is suited for courses touching on social movements, civil rights, or the 1960s. His curriculum, put in place after successful teacher workshops on gay and lesbian issues, has been taught at the public high school in Cambridge, Massachusetts, for several years.

In some schools these issues are included in a family life or sex education curriculum. But this, says Lipkin, can limit discussion of homosexuality to sexual topics and ignore the roles of gay people in society. "Offering a separate course on gay and lesbian issues is problematic as well," he adds. "Fear of being labeled and stigmatized may make both gay and straight students afraid to take the course, and the homophobic students it seeks to sensitize are highly unlikely to enroll."

Fist Fights and Death Threats

Some teachers may hesitate to raise the issue of homosexuality for fear of inciting controversy. Even in the most tolerant school districts, discussion and compromise may be needed before parents, teachers, and other members of the school community feel comfortable with lessons about gay and lesbian people.

The recent uproar in New York City over Chancellor Joseph Fernandez's multicultural "Children of the Rainbow" curriculum guide, which recommended teaching children about gays and lesbians as early as first grade, underscores the political hazards of tackling this issue. The controversy became so explosive that fist fights broke out at school board meetings. Fernandez was accused of promoting sodomy for six-year-olds, received hate mail and death threats, and ultimately lost his job—though the "Rainbow" curriculum was not the only reason for his dismissal.

Those who oppose education about gays and lesbians express a variety of fears and objections. One is that homosexuality is immoral and should not be encouraged by schools. A second objection is that the presence of gay and lesbian teachers and tolerance of homosexuality will cause otherwise straight adolescents to become gay. But research suggests that a person's sexual orientation is established at an early age and cannot be altered in this way. A review of more than 30 studies comparing children of homosexual parents with children of heterosexual parents showed no significant differences in how the children defined their own sexual identity.

Some parents worry that a gay or lesbian teacher or coach will be likely to molest students. Research does not seem to support this fear. Studies show that most sexual abuse occurs within the family. Abuse outside the family is usually committed by pedophiles, and there is no evidence that gay and lesbian adults are more likely than heerosexuals to be pedophiles.

Still, educators who want to create a more comfortable environment for gay students while enlightening heterosexual students should be prepared to face these common arguments and fears. Because of the practical difficulties of challenging deeply held values and beliefs about homosexuality, teachers may want to start with subtler ways of introducing the topic. For example, an English teacher may acknowledge that a writer being read by the class is gay or lesbian and ask students to discuss how this has affected the writer's work. This sends a signal to students that their own writing about issues of sexual identity would be acceptable. Gay and lesbian students are more likely to explore their emotions and identity confusion in writing classes if the teacher creates a welcoming and safe environment by stating and strictly enforcing a policy of confidentiality in personal essays.

Support Groups

Some schools are establishing support groups for gay and lesbian teenagers. There is no national estimate of how many such groups exist, but the movement is small and most groups have been formed within the past five years.

Before setting up such a group, a school should go through "sensitizing" steps such as workshops and training. Educators emphasize the importance of raising awareness first to build a base of support; otherwise controversy and political roadblocks may make progressive steps impossible.

There are national models for such groups. The best-known program is Uribe's Project 10 at Fairfax High School in West Hollywood, California. Founded in 1984, Project 10 provides in-school counseling and information for students, sponsors "rap" groups, and steers kids towards youth programs and university groups that welcome gay high school students so that, as Uribe puts it, "they don't end up in the bars." Staff members also conduct workshops on gay and lesbian issues for teachers and other adults.

"We are starting at ground zero," Uribe says. "We are starting to see these groups spring up, but most kids are still isolated from any source of support. And a lot of attempts to address these issues in an enlightened way are met with resistance."

Those who have set up support groups at their schools agree on some basic principles. One is that groups should be open to all students, regardless of sexual orientation. Many schools have chosen the name Gay/Straight Alliance, intending the group to educate heterosexual students, to provide support for their homosexual peers, and to be a nonthreatening place for students confused about their sexuality. Also, group members should never be asked to reveal their sexual orientation, and a person's sexual identity should never be assumed.

Scarce Role Models

Most advocates agree that gay and lesbian teachers who are open about their sexual orientation can be extremely helpful to homosexual teenagers. But the great majority of gay and lesbian teachers are staying in the closet.

Kevin Jennings, a gay teacher at Concord Academy near Boston, started GLISTEN (Gay and Lesbian School Teacher Network), which brings together gay and straight teachers to work against homophobia in both public and private schools. The group, founded in 1991, has a mailing list of over 700.

Jennings believes that gay and lesbian teachers can be an effective source of support for teenagers, but that schools cannot rely on these teachers alone. The responsibility to acknowledge the existence of gay and lesbian people and to provide a safe place for homosexual and sexually confused teens to be true to themselves, he asserts, should be shared by all educators.

"There is a crisis of gay and lesbian youth," says Jennings. "We have a responsibility to promote the emotional well-being of our students. If we don't do that for these kids, learning will be the last thing on their minds."

For Further Information

Aaron Fricke. *Reflections of a Rock Lobster: A Story about Growing Up Gay.* Boston: Alyson Publications, 1981.

GLISTEN (Gay and Lesbian School Teacher Network), c/o ISAM, 222 Forbes Rd., Suite 105, Braintree, MA 02184; 617-849-3080.

Karen Harbeck, ed. *Coming Out of the Classroom Closet: Gay and Lesbian Students, Teachers, and Curricula.* Binghamton, NY: Harrington Park Press, 1992. Factual information about gay and lesbian issues, adolescent development, and ways to address the needs of these students.

Hetrick Martin Institute. 401 West St., New York, NY 10014; 212-633-8920. Offers a range of educational and social services and is a model for other agencies. Workshops for teachers, counselors, and other educators.

Arthur Lipkin, Gay and Lesbian Curriculum and Staff Development Project, 210 Longfellow Hall, Cambridge, MA 02138; 617-495-3441 or 617-547-2197. Curriculum materials, reading lists, and staff development manuals for educators.

NEA Gay and Lesbian Caucus, P.O. Box 314, Roosevelt, NJ 08555. 609-448-5215.

Project 10, 7850 Melrose Ave., Los Angeles, CA 90046. Contact: Virginia Uribe, 818-577-4553.

Gary Remafedi. "Homosexual youth; a challenge to contemporary society." *Journal of the American Medical Association,* 258 (July 10, 1987).

Serving Gay and Lesbian Youths: The Role of Child Welfare Agencies. Washington, DC: Child Welfare League of America, 1991.

Notes on Contributors

Lisa Birk, a former teacher and counselor, is a freelance writer and editor in Boston.

Susan Eaton, a doctoral candidate at the Harvard Graduate School of Education, is assistant director and project editor for the Harvard Project on School Desegregation and coauthor, with Gary Orfield, of a forthcoming book on desegregation policy.

Helen Featherstone, founding editor of the *Harvard Education Letter,* is associate professor of teacher education at Michigan State University. She is the author of *A Difference in the Family: Life with a Disabled Child* and coeditor, with Sharon Feiman-Nemser, of *Exploring Teaching: Reinventing an Introductory Course.*

Richard Fossey is associate professor of education at Louisiana State University in Baton Rouge.

Gus Frias, a former Los Angeles police officer, is a member of the Advisory Committee on School Violence of the California Commission on Teacher Credentialing, a technical expert for the National School Safety Center, and a criminal justice specialist at the Los Angeles County Office of Education.

Edward Miller is editor of the *Harvard Education Letter* and coauthor, with Nancy Ames, of *Changing Middle Schools: How to Make Schools Work for Young Adolescents.*

Marc Posner conducts research in health promotion and risk prevention at Education Development Center in Newton, Massachusetts, and is the author of *Working Together for Youth.*

Adria Steinberg was editor of the *Harvard Education Letter* from 1988 to 1993, and is the author of *Adolescents and Schools: Improving the Fit* and coauthor, with Bruce Astrein and James W. Fraser, of *Our Children at Risk: The Crisis in Public Education.* She is currently academic coordinator of the Rindge School of Technical Arts in Cambridge, Massachusetts.